St cat

W9-CMG-814

MILK
GLASS

Lavender Ram's Head Bowl: A rare color and a rare pattern combine to make this beautiful lavender Milk Glass Bowl. I have seen this museum piece in light blue and in black but never in milk white, although I assume it was made in white. The handsome Ram's Head handles were copied from an early English china bowl.

Black Swan: The large Black Swan (Deep Amethyst) is one of the largest pieces of Milk Glass ever produced measuring 11¾" long, 7¼" high to curve of neck and 6" across. The design detail of the feathers is well executed, and the general proportions of the bird are good. The exact age of this piece is undetermined. The only other black swan of this size I have ever encountered came from the home of President James J. Garfield.

Purple Slag Celeries: Some difficulty was encountered in getting the exact purple coloring in this photograph of the two Purple Slag pieces. The darker piece on the left is of English origin easily discernible by its fine detail and deep, almost black coloring. The celery on the right is in the ever popular Fluted Pattern, a favorite design of Challinor Taylor and Company of Tarentum, Pa. This American piece had a good mix of purple and white and is a fine example of Purple Slag.

Blue Robin on Nest and Jewel Vase: Two lovely shades of blue Milk Glass are shown. The graceful Jewel Pattern vase or celery is a fine example of the darker blue occasionally encountered in Milk Glass. This shade is much rarer than the light blue of the adjoining piece. The lighter covered dish is Westmoreland's reproduction of the famous Vallerystahl Robin On The Nest.

E. McCAMLY BELKNAP

MILK

GLASS

INTRODUCTION BY
GEORGE S. McKEARIN

CROWN PUBLISHERS, Inc. • NEW YORK

PRINTED IN THE UNITED STATES OF AMERICA

SEVENTH PRINTING, JULY, 1974

To

BETTY MURROW BELKNAP

*whose companionship, understanding
and loyalty provided the inspiration
for this book*

Foreword

MY INTEREST in glass collecting began as far back as 1920. As a traveling salesman I was bored with hotel lobbies and the other usual pursuits of this genus of mankind. During one of those long, lonesome evenings I stopped at an antique shop where I became wholly absorbed. Before long I was spending my evenings chatting with antique dealers and browsing through their shops.

Not long afterward I met and became friendly with Ruth Webb Lee and George McKearin. This led to a few chores for these collectors—unearthing a choice piece of Stoddard, a rare Lily Pad Wash Bowl and Pitcher or a stray piece of Saratoga glass for Mr. McKearin; coming upon a beautiful Diamond Thumb Print Compote, a Comet Water Pitcher or an Argus Covered Sugar for Ruth Lee.

By the time the press of business activities allowed me to concentrate more seriously on my collecting, Ruth Webb Lee was recognized as the foremost authority on pressed glass and George McKearin as fount of all knowledge for early American blown glass. Since I had always been interested in Milk Glass and occasionally found pieces unlisted by Millard in *Opaque Glass* or Ruth Lee in the Milk Glass chapters of *American Pressed Glass,* I began to take this phase of the glass world very seriously. My own collection began to grow until it reached today's size of between 1200 and 1300 pieces, most of which were gathered during the past five years.

In this book, using the best possible photographs to give the reader a chance to see the important Milk Glass pieces, I have tried to cover the field completely. The kindness of many collectors made it possible to include pieces which I do not own. I have no doubt that many more Milk Glass pieces exist, but at the present writing they are unknown to me.

I have attempted to retain the names already in existence wherever possible, even if I felt that in some instances they were misnomers. I believe that it is better to carry them on, rather than to add confusion by a new appellation which differs from one used by Mrs. Lee, Mrs. Kamm or Mr. Millard. However, I am naming those pieces which are being shown for the first time, and here I have tried to be as accurately descriptive as possible.

Among collectors it has been debated whether Milk Glass includes other than milk-white pieces. Over 80% of the glass portrayed here is milk white. In recent years the various opaque glass pieces in blue, green, black and most other opaque colors have been referred to in the antique shops and by collectors as blue Milk Glass, green Milk Glass, black Milk Glass, etc.

Caramel glass, purple slag, and custard glass are called by their respective names, but are close kinfolk to the Milk Glass family and are therefore shown and catalogued under the same general family association in this book.

Originally the only true Milk Glass was milk white, but times and customs change and authors must of necessity keep up with them.

Not all Milk Glass was made in America. The better English pieces rate high among the finest Milk Glass produced, as a result of exquisite detail, beautiful chalk whiteness, and excellent proportions. French pieces, especially those produced at the Vallerystahl factory, have a marked muddy grayish cast to their appearance and lack the sharpness of detail found in the better English and American pieces. There is a tendency to use rounded corners and curves rather than straight lines and points. French pieces are usually big with the main subject supplemented by other material. For example, the background for a Milk Glass hunting dog includes a hunting pouch, a gun and forest leaves.

The only definitely French piece that I have ever seen that was white Milk Glass as we know milk white in the United States was a tall covered rooster compote produced during the 1920's. This piece was not the usual French grayish white and for that reason often fooled the most experienced collector as to its origin.

Recognizing reproductions of antique Milk Glass is an ability acquired only through long experience. I have devoted a great deal of time to this phase of collecting and I hope that Chapter Ten which incorporates the results of my research will prove useful to all readers of this book.

I have tried to keep my text as brief as possible and allow the photographs to speak for themselves. Here is not only a guide for the collector but a permanent record and tribute to the fine art of the craftsmen responsible for these superb Milk Glass pieces.

E. McCamly Belknap

March, 1949

Contents

Introduction

"CAM" BELKNAP and I have been friends for many years and quite naturally I have had first-hand knowledge of the remarkable collection of Milk Glass that he has assembled. Therefore, I have ample reason for writing an introductory note to this book. It is a book which will, I feel certain, be generally accepted as the most comprehensive and authoritative in its particular field.

I knew "Cam," as his friends call him, in the early days of his interest in glass, and whenever business took me to or near Syracuse I made it a special point to contact him. He usually had some particularly choice item in Early American Glass laid aside for me. He had a definite flair for the right thing.

When he moved West our personal contacts became less frequent, but I recall with great pleasure a visit to his home in Toledo about two years ago when I saw his most interesting collection of Milk Glass. On the same occasion I was privileged to see many of the beautiful photographs which are reproduced in the book. We also outlined the plan he had in mind, of which this book is the fulfillment.

The book is, unquestionably, an outstanding contribution to the literature on American Glass. The photographic reproductions are exceptionally fine and, as the Chinese say, "One see is worth 100 tells." The work which Mr. Belknap has done with regard to reproductions, as outlined in Chapter 10 of the book, is in itself a noteworthy achievement. It is also of special interest and great benefit to all collectors in the field of Milk Glass, which, as the author points out in his Foreword, has been broadened in its general application to include Opaque Pressed Wares of the same period in other colors.

GEORGE S. McKEARIN

Hoosick Falls, N. Y.

Acknowledgments

BECAUSE the photographs contribute so much that is essential to this book, an accolade goes to Harold E. Johnson for his excellent work. When a picture is complete few give thought to the work behind it—the hours of arranging, the hot spotlights, the many takeovers. Through it all, Harold Johnson never complained. Requests for a retake only brought forth a smile. And, miracle of miracles, he never cracked one piece of glass! It was indeed a pleasure to work with him and I am sure his finished pictures eloquently bespeak his ability.

My thanks also to Harold Waltz whose photographs, while not many, are splendid.

I am especially grateful to Mrs. Maude Doyle of Mt. Vernon, Ohio for allowing me to photograph her large and varied collection of covered animals.

Mrs. William Bullock of Toledo, Ohio provided genuine assistance as a result of her wide range of knowledge, her suggestions and advice, and the loan of many of her choice plates, compotes and covered animals.

Mrs. Jessie L. Peck of Parkman, Ohio provided much information and many of the pieces in my own collection.

I sincerely appreciate the information relating to book making given to me by Mrs. Minnie Watson Kamm.

I feel especially obligated to George Mc-Kearin, who, more than anyone else, is responsible for this book having been published.

The chapter on Reproductions could not have been written without the excellent cooperation of the executives of the Westmoreland Glass Company, especially that of James J. Brainard, president, and Larry T. Hamby, advertising account executive, and Mr. and Mrs. John E. Kemple of the Kemple Glass Works, East Palestine, Ohio.

Thanks are owed also to Mrs. Dale Myers, Howe, Indiana, I. M. Wiese, Silver Mine Tavern, Silver Mine, Connecticut, Mrs. D. W. Moor, Jr., Toledo, Ohio, Mrs. Glen G. Ramsey, Port Clinton, Ohio, Mrs. Van Doren, Clinton, Michigan, Mrs. Mae Curtis, Adrian, Michigan, Mrs. Norma E. Moebus, Lima, Ohio, Mrs. Lucille Hughes, Toledo, Ohio, Mrs. Bessie Mollard, Zelienople, Pennsylvania, Lucian Clark Bareham, Mercersberg, Pennsylvania, Pauline Whitaker, Adrian, Michigan, Roland E. Deitemeyer, Toledo, Ohio, Ralph Miller, Dalton, Ohio, Mildred Flachs, Piqua, Ohio, Mrs. Maude M. Haley, Toledo, Ohio, Mrs. Harry Bell, Seattle, Washington, and Cluff's Antique Shop, Columbus. Ohio.

I sincerely hope I have omitted none to whom I am indebted for lending me a piece of glass to photograph. If I have so erred, it was not intentional but rather caused by a short memory.

Bibliography

VICTORIAN GLASS	Ruth Webb Lee
EARLY AMERICAN PRESSED GLASS	Ruth Webb Lee
ANTIQUE FAKES AND REPRODUCTIONS	Ruth Webb Lee
OPAQUE GLASS	S. T. Millard
200 PATTERN GLASS PITCHERS	Minnie Watson Kamm
A SECOND 200 PATTERN GLASS PITCHERS	Minnie Watson Kamm
A THIRD 200 PATTERN GLASS PITCHERS	Minnie Watson Kamm
A FOURTH PITCHER BOOK	Minnie Watson Kamm
A FIFTH PITCHER BOOK	Minnie Watson Kamm
THUMBNAIL SKETCHES	J. Stanley Brothers, Jr.
THE LORE OF OUR LAND IN GLASS	Bessie M. Lindsey

MILK
GLASS

WHERE more than one piece appears on a page the arrangement is as follows: *a* is the upper left piece, *b* the upper right, *c* appears below *a, d* below *b, e* below *c* and *f* below *d*.

WHENEVER a number is preceded by an * the piece so designated has been or is being reproduced. The reproductions in Chapter Ten are not so marked.

Unless otherwise credited all pieces photographed for this book are in the Belknap collection.

Chapter One

Milk Glass Plates

PROBABLY the most popular collector's items in Milk Glass are the hundred or more patterns of Milk Glass plates. There are flower plates, children's plates, lacy-edge plates, comic plates, historical plates, bird plates, geometric-design plates, and also just plain Milk Glass plates. With such a variety to choose from, collectors can satisfy their wildest whims.

Shown on the pages of this chapter are many plates neither heretofore photographed nor previously written about by the earlier authors, Ruth Webb Lee or the late S. T. Millard.

It has been the present author's good fortune during the course of his collecting to have unearthed a number of unknown or previously undiscovered patterns in Milk Glass plates. Several of the rarer and more unusual are:

> the Painted-Bird-Center on the large Lattice-Edge Plate
> the little 5½" Lacy-Edge Fuzzy Dog plate
> the very rare Heart-in-Club plate
> the Maple-Leaf-and-Branch-Border plate
> the Half-Pinwheel plate
> the hard to find Gothic-and-Chain-Border plate
> the small Lily-of-the-Valley-Border plate
> the Roger-Williams-Memorial-Center plate

> the exquisite Chrysanthemum-Center plate
> the Square Leaf-and-Open-Scroll-Border plate.

These select patterns are new to the collector and dealer alike in that they have not been shown in other books. There are other little-known plates shown in this chapter, but the ten listed above are outstanding.

The aristocrats of the Milk Glass plate world, the items most sought after by collectors, are the large 10¼" Lattice-Edge plates, with both open or closed lattice-work edges. These handsome pieces come most often in white and only occasionally in blue. The large white ones invariably have handpainted flowers as the center motif. Popular handpainted flower designs are: Apple Blossom, Trumpet Vine, Wild Rose, and Wild Flower.

There are several plates with attractive geometric designs in the center. These are more rare than the flower centers.

Rarer still is a series of bird paintings beautifully executed in bright bird colorings, one bird to the plate. Only one of these rare Painted-Bird-Center plates is shown in this chapter. Mrs. William Bullock claims to have seen one with a red bird center and another with a blue jay.

The blue Lattice-Edge plates which have unpainted or unadorned centers are even more rare. These kings of the realm of platedom now decorate the finest opaque glass collections. To own a service setting of eight of these majestic pieces is a thrill few collectors can afford. Credit for the creation of these beautiful plates goes to the Atterbury Company of Pittsburgh, Pennsylvania.

In addition to the very rare plates described above, there are scores of others interesting to the collector.

The use of white as the predominating color in the production of Milk Glass plates was responsible for the popular term "Milk White Glass," but other colors were used as well. In quantity manufactured, second to white comes deep amethyst, often called black because the coloring is so deep in tone that it appears black unless the plate is held directly in front of the light so that the true amethyst color may be seen. Closely following comes a lovely light blue intermingled with a few off-shades of blue, some lighter and some darker than the basic color. Occasionally a chartreuse green has appeared on the collector's horizon; this is a rare shade to be found in plates, but it is not overly popular among collectors.

Many Milk Glass plates are now being reproduced. For a complete list of such plates, see Chapter Ten on "Reproductions," in which I have listed all presently known plate patterns that are being reproduced.

*1. *Washington Thirteen-Star Plate:* A scarce 8¼″ plate seldom found these days. In years of collecting I have seen only two. The plate consists of a thirteen-star border, a large head of George Washington in the center, and a facsimile of Washington's signature. *G. Washington* is under the head; the date of his birth, *1732,* and the date of his death, *1799,* appear at the base in sizable numerals. Reproduced by Westmoreland.

2a. *Geometric Design Lattice-Border Plate:* This is one of the large lattice-edge plates, approximately 10½″ in diameter from tip to tip of the lattice edges. These aristocrats of the Milk Glass plate world are most sought after by collectors and at all times bring a premium price. The blue and gold make an exquisite painted center. *From Cluff's Antique Shop Collection, Columbus, Ohio.*   2b. *Lacy Edge:* This pattern was limited to two sizes, 7½″ and 8″ diameters, with an attractive border and a plain center. It is found in blue and white.

7

3a. *Small-and-Large-Triangle Border:* Of questionable age, 7¼″ diameter. 3b. *Leaf and Branch Border:* 7¼″ in diameter, with a flower painted center. More often used as a wall piece. 3c. *Easter Bunny and Egg Plate:* One of a series of juvenile Easter Greeting plates in the usual 7¼″ diameter size. 3d. *Strawberry Plate.* When found, this entire plate was painted a light green. 3e. *Rooster and Hens Plate:* This comes in white only and in child's size, 7¼″ diameter. 3f. *Easter Rabbits Plate:* A child's 7¼″ white plate with the word *Easter* across the top.

*4a. *Shell and Club Border:* Here is a 7¼″ diameter plate in milk white. It also comes in blue and in 7¼″, 8½″, 9″, and 9½″ sizes. Presumed to be a product of the Canton Glass Company. 4b. *Gothic:* Here is a plate made by Canfield in 5½″, 7″, 7½″, 8¼″, 9″, and 9¼″ diameters during the 1890's. It was produced in white, blue and black. 4c. *Quarter-Circle Border:* This is a solid 8¼″ plate. 4d. *Shell and Grapes:* This plate has a marked opalescence in its coloring. The maker unknown, probably a fairly late vintage. *4e. *Niagara Falls Plate:* Fairly common up to several years ago but rare today. 4f. *Lacy-Edge Indian:* Millard calls this plate *Lacy-Edge Indian.* Since this name seems to have been accepted by the trade, I will avoid confusion by using it too

5a. *Columbus Plate:* A handsome 9½″ milk white plate. In the center is the bust of Columbus with *1492* and *1892* on the shoulders. A club and shell border encircles the plate. 5b. *Leaf and Scroll Square-Edge Plate:* Its delicate, easily broken edge may account for the rarity of this plate, which is 7¼″ in diameter. I have seen it in white only, but it may come in blue. 5c. *Triangle S:* This plate was designed for appearance rather than utility, for it is too easily broken. Rather scarce, it is most commonly found in the 8″ size, more often in white than blue.

6a. *Pansy Plate Round:* 7¼″ beautifully executed in milk white only.   *6b. *Cupid and Psyche:* A perfectly dead-white plate with good lines, 7½″ in diameter, an excellent example of the ornamental Milk Glass plates of the 80's. 6c. *Bryan Plate:* This plate has much fiery opalescence to it. It is 7″ in diameter.   6d. *Eagle, Flag, and Star Border:* I know of four plates featuring this border. A 7″ plate of slightly muddy Milk Glass.   6e. *Hare and Clover Leaf Plate:* 7½″ in diameter, milk white.   6f. *Yoked Slatted Border:* Fairly rare, comes in 7½″, seen in white only. Very fragile border.

*7a. *Rabbit and Horseshoe Plate:* A 7½″ child's plate, white or blue. 7b. *Owl Lovers Plate:* A small 7″ plate, in white only. 7c. *Easter Sermon:* A child's plate of 7½″, milk white. 7d. *Easter Opening:* 7½″. The words Easter Opening appear at the bottom. *7e. *Wicket Border Plate:* In the Wicket design the vertical line comes down below the cross bar; in the H pattern the vertical line halts at the cross bar. Attributed to Atterbury. Comes in 7″, 7½″, 8″, 8½″, and 9″, milk white, blue, black, and chartreuse green. 7f. *Angel Head Plate:* Sizes, 7½″, 8½″, and 9″. Colors, blue and white.

8a. *Leaf Plate:* 5½″ x 7¼″. Brilliant opalescent fire. 8b. *Grape Leaf Plate:* 6½″. Milk white glass. 8c. *Scroll and Waffle Border Plate:* Comes in 7″ and 8″. Design is solid rather than the usual open-work. 8d. *Diamond and Shell Border Plate:* An 8″ heavy plate in milk white and occasionally blue. 8e. *A.B.C. Alphabet plate:* 7″, in white and blue with beaded edge. *8f. *Beaded Loop, Indian-Head Plate:* Found in 7½″ and 8″ in white. It is not known whether or not the center Indian head represents any particular chief.

9a. *Scroll and Eye:* Attributed to Challinor, Taylor & Co. Comes in white, black, and blue. Sizes, 7¼″, 8″, 9″, and 10″. 9b. *Gothic:* Sizes, 5½″, 7″, 7¼″, 8½″, 9″, and 9¼″. Made by Canton Glass Co., in milk white, light blue, and black. 9c. *William Howard Taft Plate:* Probably a campaign plate when Taft was running against Bryan. 7″. 9d. *Jolly Friar Plate:* 7″. The muddy white glass may have resulted from in-sufficient cryolite. 9e. *The Serenade Plate:* A beautiful little 6½″ white plate made by the Indiana Tumbler and Goblet Co. *From the collection of Mrs. D. W. Moor, Jr., Toledo, Ohio.* 9f. *Lily of the Valley Border:* This 6½″ plate has a milk whiteness so often found in English pieces. With no record of manufacture I will claim that it is American made.

10a. *Block Border Deep:* Not rare, comes in white and blue and in 7½", 8½", and 9" sizes. 10b. *Flower Bordered Plate:* 7½". No outstanding details. *10c. *Three Kittens Plate:* One of the cheapest Milk Glass pieces on the market at present because of the flood of reproductions. 7". *10d. *Three Owls Plate:* A 7" child's plate with conventional looped border half way around the plate. White only. *10e. *Fleur de Lis Border:* White Milk Glass, unusually attractive, 7¼" only. *10f. *Club-Shell and Loop, Plain Center:* Popular in the 80's, this pattern comes in white or blue and in 7¼", 8½", 9", and 9½" diameters.

11a. *Stanchion Border Plate:* One of the loveliest open-edge-border plates. Black, blue and milk white, 7″ and 8½″, made by Challinor, Taylor & Co. 11b. *Hearts and Anchors:* A rare 8″ plate. *11c. *Angel and Harp:* 8″, white only, with a single-row forget-me-not border. Although the instrument is not a harp, I will retain the established name. 11d. *Single Forget-Me-Not:* Milk white, 8″, dainty, not too expensive. 11e. *Keyhole Border Plate:* A reasonably common Milk Glass plate, found in blue, black, and white, in 5½″, 6½″, 8″, and 9″ sizes. 11f. *Club and Shell, Waffle Center:* Blue or white limited to 7″ and 8¼″. Unusually heavy for its size.

12a. *Roger Williams Memorial Plate:* This is a commemorative plate and a good one. 7″, white only. Often besmirched with plenty of paint. *12b. *Contrary Mule:* A good border with a poor center subject, 7″ white. 12c. *Fan and Circle Round:* The name of this pattern presents a problem because of the different appellations given to the border parts previously. The small flare parts have been called "fans," "petals," and "shells," and the little round connecting parts have been referred to as "rings," "circles," and "loops." I shall call this 8″ milk white plate Fan and Circle. 12d. *Fan and Circle Square:* A fairly large plate with a beautiful milk whiteness to the glass. *12e. *Ancient Castle Plate:* I will continue to use Millard's name *Ancient Castle* for this 7″ plate even though close examination proves it is not a castle. 12f. *Keyhole Variant:* An uncommon plate, 7¼″, milk white only.

*13a. *Anchor and Yacht:* A different 7¼″ white Milk Glass plate. Created and still being made by Westmoreland. 13b. *Dart Border:* This pattern looks for all the world like a beautiful snowflake. 7¼″, in milk white and blue. 13c. *101 Border:* This 101 pattern has been found in white and in blue, and has been heard of in black. The sizes known are 5½″, 7½″, 8¼″, and 9″ diameters. 13d. *Hearts and Clubs Border:* An exquisite pattern in white only, 8½″. Very rare. *13e. *Heart Border:* Made by the Canton Glass Co., in 6″, 8″, and 10″; in milk white, blue, or black. 13f. *Woof Woof Plate:* 5½″, blue and white.

14a. *Backward C Square:* A rare example of the square Milk Glass plate with the Backward C border. 8″. 14b. *Backward C. Round:* The *Backward C* is one of the choicest of the open-edge plates. It is found in white, blue, and black, and in 7″, 8″, 8½″, and 10″. A variant of the regular *Round C.* Close observation will show the difference—the top of the C at the outer edge in this piece has no little knob as does the regular *Backward C.* 14c. *Crown Border:* A heavy plate with a very gingerbready border. 7½″, in white only. 14d. *Leaf Plate:* 6″. Usually found covered with green paint. 14e. *Chrysanthemums Plate:* This could be a French piece as it has a small double fleur de lis motif at one side. However, it is the chalky white of English Milk Glass instead of the muddy gray of French glass. I doubt if it is an American piece. 14f. *Setting Hen and Chicks Plate:* A juvenile Easter plate, blue or white, 7¼″.

15a. *Easter Verse Plate:* The center is decorated and lettered by hand. Note the intricate detail of the flower and lettering decoration. 15b. *Sunken Rabbit Plate:* The rabbit is depressed below the surface rather than raised above it, as in ill. 6e. In white only. *15c. *Small Pinwheel Plate:* These really beautiful plates are rare. Only in white, and in 7″, 8″, 10″. 15d. *Backward C Round Plate:* This is an excellent example of stamp decoration. Many Milk Glass plates were decorated with U. S. postage stamps. The border pattern made no difference as long as the plate had a smooth center for mounting the stamps. 15e. *Single Forget-Me-Not Plate:* Excellent example of a painted plate. *From the Lucille Hughes Collection, Toledo, Ohio.* *15f. *Yacht and Anchor Plate:* Another example of a painted plate with gold chain border *From the Lucille Hughes Collection, Toledo, Ohio.*

Gothic, it has slightly rounded edges instead of the pointed edges usually associated with this pattern. Second, the border design is beaded on the surface, not plain as in the best known Gothic pattern. Third, part of the open-work border is open and part is solid because of carelessness in filling the mold during manufacture. Fourth, the center has an excellent design of the bust of William Jennings Bryan.

16a. *Black Forget-Me-Not:* A rather striking black Milk Glass Triple-Row Forget-Me-Not 9″ plate, produced by the Canton Glass Co. The running stag painted in white in the center is executed so professionally it is presumed to have been done at the factory. Black plateware is not decorated as often as white. 16b. *Beaded Gothic Border with Bryan Center:* This Gothic Border plate in black Milk Glass is shown for several reasons. First, although the border is

17a. *Flower-in-Square Plate:* The pattern is entirely on the under side of this 7¼″ opalescent plate. The top or usable surface is as plain-faced as a spinster without makeup. Many attractive pieces feature the pattern on the bottom rather than the upper surface, a fact I have never been able to explain. 17b. *Arch Border Plate:* Challinor, Taylor & Co. created this beautiful pattern. It comes in 6″, 8″, 9″, and 10¼″ sizes. Millard states: "They sometimes have a dull appearance due to the use of tin oxide in the mix instead of cryolite." But the majority I have found are a beautiful milk white. 17c. *Daisy Band and Roman Key Plate:* A rare, fiery opalescent 6″ plate with an upsidedown complex. This is a truly beautiful little plate, with its intricate pattern work on the underneath side. About these two plates: where they were made, in what period, and by whom, is not known.

18. *Morning Glory Pinwheel Plate:* This is a fine example of the large Pinwheel plates produced by Challinor, Taylor and Company of Tarentum, Pennsylvania. The painted centers of these beautiful plates were done by true artists who took pride in their work and accordingly turned out praiseworthy work. These plates are definitely rare, collectors' pieces, priced in the upper brackets. The center painting is the morning glory. *From the collection of Mrs. William Bullock, Toledo, Ohio.*

19. *Field Flowers Pinwheel Plate:* Another large pinwheel border plate with a field flower hand-painted center. These plates, lovely beyond description, can scarcely be done justice to by black and white photographs. They must be seen in all their bright floral colorings to be appreciated. They seem to vary slightly in the large sizes, from 10¼″ to 10½″ in diameter. Proud indeed should be the hostess who serves her guests from a set of these Milk Glass rarities. *From the collection of Mrs. William Bullock, Toledo, Ohio.*

20a. *Half-Pinwheel Plate:* Another unpublished plate of rare design. White and 8″ only. 20b. *Gothic and Chain Border:* A rare and previously unnamed Milk Glass plate. 8¼″, milk white. 20c. *Three Puppies Plate:* The unique open leaf border is found only on this and 20d. 20d. *Dog and Cats Plate:* 6″, white; probably used as a wall plaque. 20e. *Block Border Fancy:* This Fancy has a scroll-like edge to the border. Blue or white, 7″, 8¼″, and 9″. 20f. *Block Border Plain:* All the Block Border patterns, of which there are several, have a fairly deep recessed center. White or blue, 7½″, 8½″, 9″ sizes.

21a. *The Little Red Hen Plate:* 7¼″, either white or blue.　21b. *Chick and Eggs Plate:* Juvenile Easter plate, 7¼″, blue or white. *21c. *Triple Forget-Me-Not Plate:* Produced by the Canton Glass Co., in 7″, 8¼″, and 9″, in white, blue, and black.　21d. *Horseshoe and Anchor Plate:* Probably a wall plaque. On the back is patent date, *December 10, 1901.* 7¾″ top to bottom and 6½″ at its widest. *From the collection of Mrs. Pauline Whitaker, Adrian, Michigan.*　21e. *Painted Flower Border:* 7½″. White only (with a bluish tint). Deep. Background is unusual fishnet weave.　21f. *Pussy Cat Plate:* A souvenir from the Mansfield (Pennsylvania) Fair of 1901. It had the popular gilt border. 7¼″.

22. *Trumpet Vine Pinwheel Plate:* Another example of the famous Pinwheel flower hand-painted center plates for your inspection. Each of these large Pinwheel plates seems to have a personality of its own. All of them are rarities and I am sure true collectors will want to see the different flower centers created by the artists of Challinor, Taylor. These large Pinwheel plates are placed in the same collectors' category as the famous Lattice-edge plates made by the Atterbury Company of Pittsburgh, Pennsylvania. *From the collection of Mrs. William Bullock, Toledo, Ohio.*

23. *Open-Lattice Conventional Design:* Another Atterbury beauty, with a conventional flower design. I understand these plates originally sold for 89¢ each. But I presume that was back in the days of 15¢-a-dozen eggs, 5¢ shoe shines, and a-dollar-a-day paychecks. Note that the thickness of the lattice-edge varies in different plates. This plate shows a very heavy lattice-edge, while the lattice work of the Trumpet Vine Lattice-edge Plate (Illustration 25) is quite fragile. *From the collection of Mrs. William Bullock, Toledo, Ohio.*

24a. *Spring Meets Winter Plate:* I looked a year to find this plate which is not too easily found these days. Of fair Milk Glass quality, it is 7¼" in diameter. 24b. *Queen Victoria Plate:* A rare and interesting Club and Fan Border plate, this has a likeness of Queen Victoria in the center. The name *Victoria R* is directly underneath the head and shoulder figure of the queen. The plate is 7" in diameter. 24c. *Mother Goose Plate:* The small Mother Goose 6¼" plate is good white Milk Glass. 24d. *Easter Ducks Plate:* This comes in 6¼" and 7½" sizes, in very poor quality grayish Milk Glass. 24e. *Chicks on Wooden Shoe Plate:* 6¼" juvenile plate with the heart-shaped lacy border. 24f. *Emerging Chick:* This little plate comes in milk white and blue, in the 6¼" size only, with heart-shaped lacy-edge border.

25. *Trumpet Vine Lattice-Edge Plate:* One of the loveliest of the open-work Lattice-edge hand-painted designs is the Trumpet Vine. The picture shows every detail of this collectors' pattern, measuring 10½″ from lattice tip to lattice tip. Many of these flower decorated plates are badly worn and the flower design is nearly obliterated. To find a table setting for eight is a real achievement for any collector. *From the collection of Mrs. William Bullock, Toledo, Ohio.*

26. *Wild Rose, Closed Lattice-Edge Plate:* The famous Wild Rose handpainted design is shown here. I would like very much to have had all these Lattice-edge plates with their various flower designs reproduced in full color for the benefit of my readers. But costs did have to be considered and they do make the color plates prohibitive. The usual 10½″ size, this plate is the highest quality of Milk Glass. An Atterbury plate.

27. *Bird Painting, Closed Lattice-Edge Plate:* Black and white photography could not possibly do justice to this handpainted Bird-Center-Plate. The bird coloring is truly a work of art. These bird paintings are the choicest collectibles of all the Milk Glass plates and are very rare. They probably at one time came in complete sets. Mrs. Bullock has seen a red bird and a blue jay, and there must be others. Note the painted circle inside the border: plates come with or without this circle. This is a 10½″ plate. *From the collection of Mrs. William Bullock, Toledo, Ohio.*

Chapter Two

Candlesticks and Lamps

COMPARATIVELY few milk white or opaque glass candlesticks were manufactured; lamps by the hundreds of thousands—but not so the candlestick. Crucifix candlesticks, however, were made in a variety of sizes and designs. Three pairs are shown in this chapter, and I have seen three or four different pairs in other collections.

It seems that in the 1870's, after the War Between the States, there was a definite religious revival during which a number of Milk Glass religious candlesticks were produced. But the great majority that I have examined personally could lay claim to no such early ancestry.

Two unusually exquisite pairs of candlesticks attributed to Sandwich are called to your attention in this chapter: the pair of genuine Petticoat-base Dolphins and the stately pair of Loop and Petal. (It is known beyond question that these two Milk-Glass-style candlesticks were products of the Sandwich factory.)

Both the Dolphin and the Loop and Petal candlesticks were manufactured in milk white. In the Loop and Petal, I have seen not only the all-white pictured in this chapter, but also blue bases and clambroth (grayish) tops, blue bases and white tops and vice versa.

Milk Glass Dolphin candlesticks came with a variety of bases (below the dolphin). Some are pyramided and square, some six-sided, and some (like the one shown later in this chapter) come with the scalloped or petticoat base. The upper parts or tops also vary. The petal tops are as common to the Dolphin base as to the Loop and Petal candlesticks. You will note that the top of

the pair of Dolphins shown in this chapter is quite different from the Loop and Petal design.

One practically foolproof method of telling the originals from the reproductions in both the Dolphin and the Loop and Petal designs is that the originals were manufactured in two pieces and annealed together. The dolphins were so joined just above the dolphin's tail. Also, in the old original candlesticks the mold marks seldom if ever line up perfectly. The workmen did not bother to match the mold lines, and so they are slightly off center. In the reproductions the mold marks match up perfectly because they are molded all in one piece.

Another really handsome pair of old-timers is the Swirl pattern design, found occasionally in clear pressed glass. They are a great rarity in Milk Glass. For a long time I sincerely doubted if they would appear in the pages of this book. The owner, who acquired them from her grandmother, named them the cause of her starting her own Milk Glass collection. No fond parent ever guarded her first offspring with greater care and caution. It took over a year of masterful eloquence to get her permission to photograph them away from home; and even then, it was almost necessary to promise an escort of a squad of state police to guard the precious darlings to the photographer and back! I don't blame her, though.

Milk white seems to have been the predominating color used in making candlesticks. I do not recall ever having seen a pair in old black glass, although in the 1920's the dime stores had a rash of 50¢-a-pair black candlesticks and did a land-office business for a few months on these illegitimate offspring of some profit-happy glass house. Currently, reproductions in black are being made.

I have yet to see a pair colored green, gray, or yellow. I have seen a stray pair or two in purple slag and on occasion have unearthed a blue pair. In Boston last summer I came upon a stunning pair of blown blue Milk Glass candlesticks—beautiful beyond description. Since the price tag of $125 for the pair put a marked damper on my enthusiasm, this book will do without them.

The unusual pair of blue candlesticks which does appear in this chapter will bear close examination. The lines and contours of this stately pair are outstanding, but frankly, I question its claim to antiquity. The pieces have a very marked nineteen-twentyish look, both in the glass content and in general appearance. They were purchased from a reputable dealer who was ready to stake her reputation on their lineage—but I am afraid she would have lost. They are not old, but they are the only examples of this exact pattern I have seen. They lack the sharp, clear outline of the genuine early pieces, and all the corners of the square tops and bases have distinct roundness that just is not found in really old glass.

Now and then you will find the flat-style candlesticks in the form of a leaf or a saucer. At other times, odds and ends will come to light, in the shape of a little alligator whose turned-up tail forms the handle, a rose blossom with a candle holder in the center, etc. Oddities all—but Milk Glass and collectible.

On the whole, Milk Glass candlesticks are rare. Choice pairs like the Sandwich Dolphins, the Sandwich Loop and Petal, or the graceful Swirl patterns are practically museum pieces.

Milk Glass lamps, on the other hand, were made in so many styles that they still exist in almost every size and description, small, large, thin, squatty, fat, high or low, minia-tures to gargantuans. Some have figures that rival Betty Grable, and others that only a fond mother could love. The illustrations in the following pages should give a fair cross section of collectible pieces.

The bases of some lamps are bronze or other metals, with Milk Glass bowls and shades to match. Some manufacturers turned out attractive models entirely in Milk Glass, the base, the bowl, all the lamp, being opaque; while still others worked out various metal-glass or glass-metal combinations. One really outstanding combination is shown, with a bronze footing: a tall blue Milk Glass base topped by a beautiful apple-shaped milk white bowl for the oil. This unusual grouping of two shades of Milk Glass—light blue and milk white—is very rare. Still other rarities are amber or blue glass (not Milk Glass) bases and exquisite ribbed Milk Glass bowls.

Occasionally lamps are found in pairs or a pair may be matched after considerable browsing, hunting, and searching. Such a pair of matched beauties are the Spanish coin lamps shown in this chapter. To own such a pair would gladden the heart of the most blasé collector. Unfortunately, the photograph of this particular pair fails to show its full beauty. The design detail of the Spanish coins could not be captured and their rare beauty of form and shape seems to elude the camera eye.

There are a great many miniature Milk Glass lamps to be found. It has always been debatable whether these were children's lamps for little girls to play with or small bedside lamps used by grown-ups. I have talked with many old folks who owned such lamps in their youth but no two seem to agree about their original use or origin. One says that her lamp was given to her at Christmas as a doll's lamp and yet another says she gave her mother one as a birthday gift to be used as a bedside lamp, so the subject seems open to argument.

28. *Dolphin Sandwich Candlesticks:* Here they are to gaze upon and admire—a pair of petticoat-base white Milk Glass Dolphin Sandwich candlesticks. There are many reproductions floating about, but these are the originals: 8¼″ tall, 4″ across the base. Annealed together in the middle, tops and bases were made in separate molds. Other bases I have seen were square and hexagonal; and another top in petal design is also attributed to Sandwich. There is no doubt that several different top and bottom combinations were manufactured.

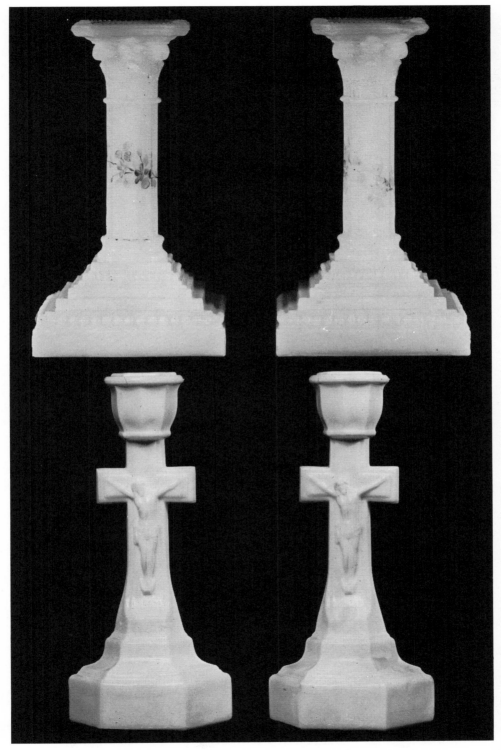

29a. *Column with Pyramid Base:* Attractive candlesticks with floral decoration around columns. 3½″ at base, 6½″ tall. Not too early. 29b. *Crucifix Candlesticks:* Extremely white Milk Glass. A definitely early appearance. 9½″ tall, unusually heavy base 3¾″ across. Horizontal bar of cross is extraordinarily thin for Crucifix candlesticks.

30a. *Crucifix Candlesticks:* This pair of small Crucifix candlesticks appear to be of French Milk Glass. By that I mean that they have a grayish off-cast coloring often found in French Milk Glass. Only 7" tall, these have a 3¼" base. The photograph gives a far better impression than the actual candlesticks warrant. Unlike most French pieces, these are not marked with the name *Vallerystahl.* 30b. *Cru-*

cifix Candlesticks: Another pair of tall, yet different Crucifix candlesticks: nearly 10" tall with a deep 4" base, these are an off-shade white—in fact, each of the pair differs slightly in whiteness from the other. The horizontal bar is relatively thick. This is definitely a late pair. Although there are many other Milk Glass religious candlesticks, the three pairs illustrated in this chapter indicate the variety.

31a. *Maple Leaf Candlestick:* An artistic yet practical little candlestick for bedside use, this piece is 6″ wide and 2½″ tall. The Maple Leaf design is excellent.   31b. *Colonial Candlestick:* The regal bearing, sharpness of detail, solidity, and color (there are touches of bluish white throughout) mark the early ancestry of this tall and handsome candlestick. It was pro-duced by the manufacturers of the early flint glass pieces of the 1850's and 60's. Its companions are Ashburton, Excelsior, and Loop. In size this is 9″ tall, footed by a 4″ base. I have scoured the country for the companion to this distinguished aristocrat (originally found in Washington, D. C.) but, to date, have never seen another. It is both early and rare.

32a. *Blue Grecian Column Candlesticks:* Tall, graceful, and a beautiful shade of blue Milk Glass best describe this pair of outstanding candlesticks. They lack the clear cut outline of the early mold-makers and the glass has a greasy appearance. They are shown here purely as a fine example of what not to purchase as an antique. 32b. *Rose Bowl Lamp:* The beautiful Rose Bowl lamp is slender and handsome, and tall enough to read by, which was not too common a feature among the old Milk Glass lamps. It has pleasing lines and is a good example of the all-white Milk Glass lamp. 32c. *Paneled Poppy:* The squat little fellow on the right is just plain lamp. It no doubt had a bowl-shaped shade to match, the same pattern as the base, but the shade was not present when the base was found. There are dozens of patterns in this style of lamp and almost as **many** shapes.

33. *Swirl Candlesticks:* This pair of oldsters is far handsomer than a picture can indicate. They are beautiful examples of good Milk Glass, very similar to the fine early flint-pressed glass Swirl candlesticks. They belonged to the grandmother of the current owner. *From the collection of Mrs. Glenn G. Ramsey, Port Clinton, Ohio.*

34. *Loop and Petal Candlesticks:* Aristocrats to the tops of their six petals, this pair of early Sandwich candlesticks is the answer to a collector's prayer. Occasionally the pattern has been found in vaseline glass, now and then in clear pressed glass, but a pair in white Milk Glass is a rarity of rarities. If you ever have closely examined pieces of the Loop pattern in Milk Glass produced at Sandwich, you will note a certain blackish tint found in no other Milk Glass. Touches of fiery opalescence often tip the edges. There are two pieces to each of these candlesticks which as a whole measure 6¾″ in height and 4½″ at the base.

35a. *Low Scroll Candleholders:* This is a pair of late candleholders, of the blue paint era. When originally found, they had a light blue paint around the base and on the handles. They measure 4¾″, with a 3¾″ base. 35b. *Climbing Rose Candlestick:* This fairly late candlestick has roses climbing up the ridges and along its 4″ base. It is 6½″ tall. Hardly a collector's choice. 35c. *Small Scroll Candlestick:* Millard calls this candlestick the *Pyramid Candleholder*. Since I have used the name "Column and Pyramid" elsewhere in this chapter, I call this pattern *Small Scroll* because of the small scroll-work. No great value as an antique. 6½″ tall with a 3¾″ base.

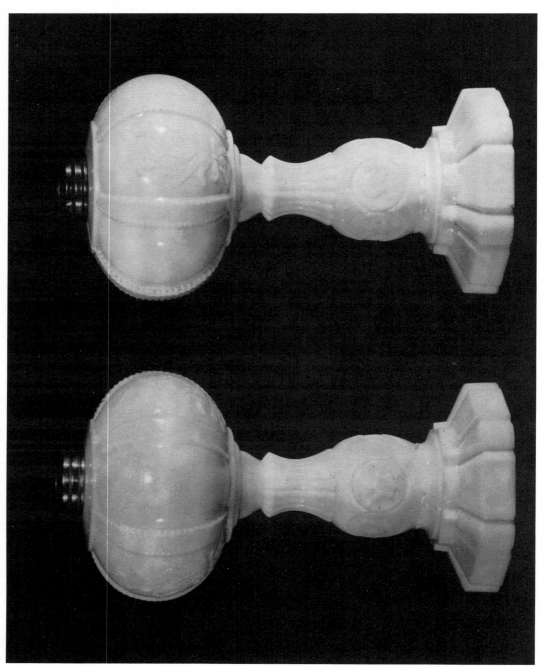

36. *Spanish Coin Lamps:* A rare and lovely pair of Milk Glass oil lamps in the well known Spanish Coin pattern. The detail on the bowls and bases of these lamps is very beautifully executed but, unfortunately, could not be caught with the camera. These are so rare that they are just not to be found on antique dealers' shelves; and I have never seen a pair in a private collection, although there un- doubtedly are a number of these lamps in existence.

37. *Octagon Base Lamp:* A lovely medium sized all-white Milk Glass lamp, this is 8¾″ tall with a base spread of 5″. The oil bowl and the octagon base were made separately, then joined together. Note the charm and grace of this hourglass figure. This style of Milk Glass lamp, eagerly sought by collectors, is usable and very easy to live with.

38a. *Paneled Pansy Lamp.* 38b. *Hourglass Candlestick:* Rare, very early, slightly grayish blown Milk Glass. 7″ tall. 38c. *Skirt Base Candlestick:* Crude, of late vintage, looks like a china candlestick. 8½″ in height.

39. *Apple Bowl with Blue Base:* No illustration can do justice to this lamp. The bowl is a lovely apple shape in white Milk Glass, while the supporting Milk Glass base is light blue. This lamp has the charm and poise of a true aristocrat and I consider it one of the choice pieces in my collection. Seldom do you find lamps with two differing colors of Milk Glass. Often there are plain white Milk Glass bases with clear or colored glass bowls, but not two colors of Milk Glass in the same lamp.

40a. *Block Lamp:* This lamp and the Miniature Block and Circle Lamp (to the right) remind me of the many mother-and-daughter advertisements in which both wear the same dresses. The Block pattern is fairly common and can still be found with little effort. It is a good looking Milk Glass lamp which should be acquired before it becomes rare. 40b. *Miniature Block and Circle Lamp:* This little Block and Circle is one of the commonest patterns found in miniature lamps. I have seen at least fifty this past year. It's a cute little lamp and makes an interesting conversational piece for any collector. It often has a little Block and Circle globe, and sometimes features a plain clear glass miniature chimney.

41. *Mae West Lamp:* Only Mae West and this Milk Glass lamp could have this figure! Or maybe this hourglass silhouette was so popular in the 1880's and 90's that the designer just copied the shape of his time. The lamp is severely plain, with not a semblance of pattern on it; all milk white, 10¼″ tall with a 6″ base and a 6″ bowl.

42. *Overlay Cranberry with Milk Glass Base:* This really stunning lamp has a beautiful white overlay over a cranberry bowl, with a column-style Milk Glass base. The lamp has a permanent home in our living room on one end of the piano. It's a tall lamp, exceptionally so—13″ in height—with a good sized 6½″ bowl. It is a fine example of a Milk Glass base used in contrast with a colored glass top or bowl.

43a. *Honeycomb Bowl with Milk Glass Base:*
A beautiful small lamp with a Honeycomb pattern clear glass bowl, this has a startling fiery opalescent Milk Glass base. A very early lamp, it is crude in construction and has an unusual base and bowl connection. The opalescent base is built up around and fastened to a nob on the bottom of the bowl. This is a rare combination of glass, truly a collectors' item. *From the collection of Ralph Miller, Dalton, Ohio.* 43b. *Clear Glass Bowl with Milk Glass Base:* What

there was to patent in this lamp, I shall never know. It is very plain, with a clear glass bowl and a Milk Glass skirt base; no design, and yet there is the notation, *Pat'd June 22nd, 1872,* under the base skirt. The entire patent wording is upside down and backwards. The bowl is built around the top of the base (just the reverse of its companion lamp, the Honeycomb Bowl shown here). This piece is 8¼″ tall, with a 5½″ clear glass bowl.

44a. *Blue Bowl with Milk Glass Base:* It is unfortunate that this photograph could not be reproduced in color. The lamp features a stunning midnight blue bowl with an entwined ribbon design skillfully worked around the complete bowl. The base is white Milk Glass. It is the contrast of dark blue and white that makes the lamp so attractive. A medium sized piece, this is 10¾" tall with an almost round 5" bowl.

44b. *Pleated Milk Glass Bowl with Amber Base:*

This Pleated Milk Glass Bowl has been found in various combinations. I have seen a white Milk Glass bowl with a purple slag base, and a white Milk Glass bowl with a blue clear base. The illustrated lamp has a pleated Milk Glass bowl and a delightful deep amber clear glass base, 10" tall. The pleated bowl is 4" in size. The lamp isn't very rare, but it is good looking and an excellent decorative piece for almost any room in the house

45a. *Loop Bowl with Milk Glass Base:* Just a good big clumsy Milk Glass base lamp with a slight list to the starboard. Nothing pretty about this lamp, unless you can call a wholesome look and matronly shape pretty. The large clear glass bowl, 6″ across and 5″ deep, would hold enough oil for a week. The height of the piece is 12¼″.
45b. *Cable, Ring, and Star Bowl with Milk Glass Base:* The bowl of this Milk Glass base lamp is a variant of the early flint glass Cable and Ring pattern. These bowls were made separately and then attached to various bases. I have a lamp with this identical bowl on a clear pressed glass base. You will note that the connecting brass couplet on this differs from that on the Loop Bowl Lamp. These seem to differ on most lamps, the ribbed one on the Loop Bowl being more common than the other.

46a. *Paneled Poppy Miniature Lamp:* This miniature Milk Glass lamp in the Paneled Poppy pattern with matching base and globe is 5¾″ in height and just less than 3″ across the base. Miniature lamps like this one are exact reproductions of the large lamps in every detail but size. 46b. *Flower Base Miniature Lamp with Clear Chimney:* This little Flower Base lamp does not have a matching globe, but instead proudly boasts a **miniature clear glass chimney.**

The illustrations of this Flower Base Miniature and of the Paneled Poppy Miniature clearly show two distinct styles: miniature lamp with a matching globe and miniature lamp with a clear glass chimney. The height of this Flower Base, chimney and all, is 7½″, and the bowl base is 2½″ wide. These miniature lamps are very much sought after by collectors and always bring good prices.

Chapter Three

Trays and Platters

THE SELECTION of choice collector's items in trays and platters is rather limited. The color variety is even more limited. No black, an occasional blue, and a few strays in green have been located (I saw a large waffle platter in chartreuse green several years ago); neither yellow, gray, nor lavender is found. Once in a while a tray in caramel glass appears, and there are several styles of trays in purple slag. Except for these few examples mentioned here, the trays and platters are white. The shadings of milk white may vary from bluish skimmed milk to grayish white, and from a stark chalk white to fiery opalescent.

Among the outstanding examples of Milk Glass platters are several worthy of special mention. The expertly designed Retriever Pattern is one of the best known and most popular patterns available to collectors. A true craftsman's work went into the creation of this delightfully executed platter. Since much of its intricate detail is lost in a photograph, you must envision the loveliness of the original. A design of large lily-pad leaves completely encircles the platter, while the center portrays a retriever ardently swimming through dense cattails in pursuit of an injured duck.

Another handsome platter is the Liberty Bell pattern of Centennial fame, 1776–1876, with a reproduction of John Hancock's signature, a large facsimile of the Liberty Bell, and the term *Declaration Independence*

in sizable letters. Across the top border in large letters also are the words *100 Years Ago*. This platter is much rarer than the Retriever, but lacks the intricate detail work.

You will find several bread trays, rather heavy, clumsy affairs, difficult to photograph because of their round edges. These fairly common trays are in the lower price bracket.

Most numerous of the trays are the varied and assorted pin or dresser trays. These come in all sizes, shapes, and descriptions, with a variety of decorations, from garlands of flowers to monkey-face corners.

A limited group of small trays was used for cigars, cigarettes, or matches. Several examples of these novelties are shown.

A good photograph of the very rare Lincoln platter or plaque is included here. The excellently detailed head of Lincoln is one of the rarest pieces of Milk Glass. I scoured the country for over five years before finding the item at an Antique Show in New York last year, and then—miracle of miracles—I located *two* in the same booth, each belonging to a different dealer. One plaque was badly cracked clear across its slat open-work border, but the other was proof. It is this latter specimen that you see in this chapter.

This Lincoln piece evidently was used as a wall plaque and not as a dish or platter, for the head of Lincoln is raised considerably above the center surface and the lattice open-work sides are too widely spaced to hold anything. Plate, platter, or plaque— it is rare, and most interesting from a collector's standpoint.

There are several unusual trays with Milk Glass centers and clear pressed glass borders. One, called *The Three Graces,* is round in shape and has handles. The one illustrated, which is oval in shape and has handles on the ends with two figures at the base of a large cross, is called the *Rock of Ages Platter.* The patent date, *November 23, 1875,* is impressed in the clear glass border.

A few small pickle or relish trays are scattered through the chapter. Some of these,

made of excellent Milk Glass of rather early vintage, differ greatly in quality from the pin and dresser trays of the '90s.

A fine photograph shows the delicate details of the rare Child and Shell Tray. Millard calls this unique piece the *Little Bo Peep Platter.* I hesitate to change a semi-established name, but frankly I think Child and Shell a more appropriate one.

This chapter pictures only the rarer pieces in Milk Glass. I have omitted the many, many additional but common items that fall under this heading.

47. *Child and Shell Tray:* A delightful small tray for candies, nuts, or relishes, this is a rare find in white Milk Glass. The size is 8¾″ by 6¼″. The little fellow reclining in the shell has been called everything from Little Bo Peep to Moses in the Bullrushes. I can't see any rushes or sheep. Can you?

48. *Fan and Circle Variant:* This handsome cake tray would make even stale cookies taste good. It is a fine example of Milk Glass, almost pure white, with a Fan and Circle border beautifully handpainted. This is unusually large for a Milk Glass piece.

49. *Lacy-Edge Cake Tray:* Delicate as a snowflake and pure white, this lacy-border cake tray is an Atterbury product worthy of its early heritage.

50. *Lincoln Plaque:* This is a good likeness of the extremely rare Lincoln Plaque. Its size, 8″ by 10½″, would indicate that it is a wall plaque rather than platter, although it is called a platter by many dealers and collectors. The raised profile of Lincoln is too high off the plate surface and covers too much of the center area, it seems to me, to let the piece be used for any practical purpose. The interwoven slat border is an interesting and unusual treatment.

51. *Liberty Bell Platter:* A fine example of a well known pressed glass pattern, this Milk Glass platter is a beauty both in clarity and in detail. The lettering is plainly readable, the bell outline well done, and the facsimile of John Hancock's signature one of the finest I have ever found in glass. The platter is 9½″ by 13½″ in size.

52. *Waffle Platter:* Quality glass, sharp detail, and good milk white coloring make the Waffle Platter a collectors' piece. This is an unusually fine example of the Waffle pattern; it is a large platter, 8½″ by 12¼″ in size. I have also found this platter in chartreuse green.

53. *The Retriever Platter:* An all-time favorite, the Retriever Platter is one of the most popular Milk Glass items. It is not too rare. I have seen a dozen or more in the antique shops this past year, and they always bring a good price. Note the lily pad border design, the hunting dog swimming through cattails and rushes, and the wounded duck trying to escape. Good interest and fast action, all in a 9¾″ by 13¼″ area.

54a. *Rock of Ages Platter:* This tray makes use of Milk Glass in an unusual manner—it has a Milk Glass top and a clear glass border and back. An overlay center of Milk Glass was applied to the clear pressed glass platter. 9″ by 13″, fairly rare. The patent date, *November 23, 1875,* is imprinted in the clear glass border. Under the two figures at the base of the cross are the words, *Rock of Ages.* At the top of the cross appears the motto, *Simply to the Cross I Cling.* 54b. *Basket Weave Bread Tray:* This is a large and fairly heavy tray, 9¾″ by 12″ in size. *Give Us This Day* is printed on the top border; *Our Daily Bread,* on the lower. The patent date, *June 30, '74,* appears on back.

55a. *Diamond Grill Bread Tray:* Because of curved surfaces and light reflection, all details of this tray could not be caught in a photograph. Nearly 10″ wide by 12″. The *Give Us This Day* on the top border does not show, but the *Our Daily Bread* at the base can be seen fairly well.

55b. *Summer Flower Dresser Tray:* This is a rather mediocre, washed out, watery Milk Glass tray, late of birth and with little to recommend it as a collectors' piece. This tray is far from rare and may be picked up for a few dollars in many antique shops. It is 8½″ by 12″ in size.

56a. *Actress Dresser Tray:* This woman's-head tray has been called by various names, among which is Millard's choice of *Lady Bust Platter.* Famous actress names, from Neilson to Lillian Russell, are used by many dealers and collectors. Since most people believe it is the head of an actress—although no one is certain who—I'll call it *Actress.* 56b. *Candlewick Tray:* The real pattern to this small tray (8½" long by 7½" across and only 1¼" deep) is on the bottom. See the chapter on bowls for the full details of the Candlewick Pattern bowl.

57. *Chrysanthemum Dresser Tray:* Most Milk Glass dresser trays are made of rather poor quality Milk Glass and are of recent origin. This is the exception: it is made of excellent quality glass and has an attractive Chrysanthemum design to boot. It is 7½″ by 10″ in size.

58. *Rose Garland Dresser Tray:* The Rose and Ribbon design of this dresser tray is daintily executed, the glass of fair quality. The edges show touches of fiery opalescence and there is a skimmed-milk bluish tinge throughout. A medium-sized tray, this measures 8¼″ by 11¼″.

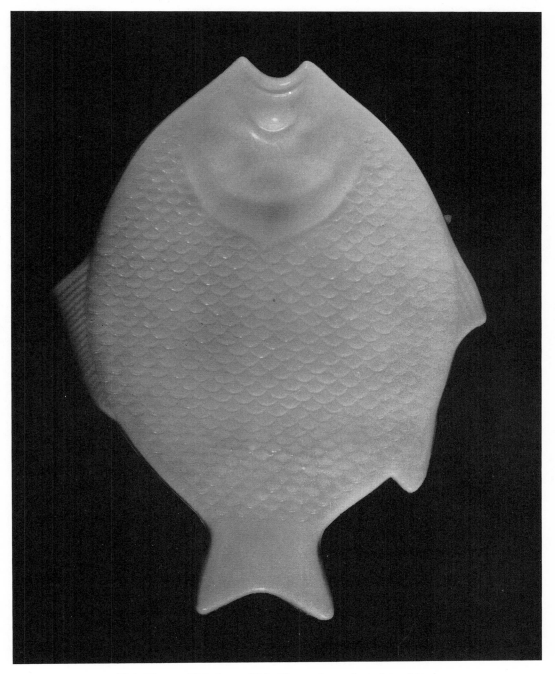

59. *Fish Platter:* This large Fish Platter is attributed to Atterbury. If this is correct, the piece is not up to the high quality of most Atterbury products. It is presumed to be a tray that goes with smaller fish trays or dishes. Some dealers call the small fish dish a pickle dish. 13¾″ long and 10½″ from fin to fin. Patent date, June 4, 1872.

60a. *Beaded Oval Tray:* One of the pin or dresser trays in an attractive shape, this tray has a beaded edge framing the garlands of flowers in the center. The flower detail is delicately designed although it does not show up to advantage in the photograph because of the depth of the piece. Of heavy glass with a slight bluish watery-milk appearance, the tray is 10″ by 7¼″ in size. 60b. *Heavy Scroll Pin Tray:* On this better-than-average dresser tray with fair glass content the design is good—heavy and mannish —just the thing for papa's collar and cuff buttons. 11¼″ long by 7″ wide, its heavy and unusual design keeps this pin tray from being commonplace. 60c. *Shell Relish Tray:* This small shell design pickle tray makes a good relish, nut, or candy dish for everyday use. 60d. *Lacy-Edge Shell Tray:* Of better glass and earlier date than the Shell Relish Tray, this is a rather ornate little Milk Glass dish, 5¼″ across (including the lacy edge) and 7¼″ in length.

61. *Lady and Fan Tray:* This is a daring subject for Victorian days. In size this tray is 7″ across the fan and 5¼″ high. It is fiery opalescent around the edges, and bluish milk white in the center. Evidently there is not enough cryolite in the mix to make it true milk white. *From the collection of Mrs. Bessie B. Mollard and Son, Zelienople, Pa.*

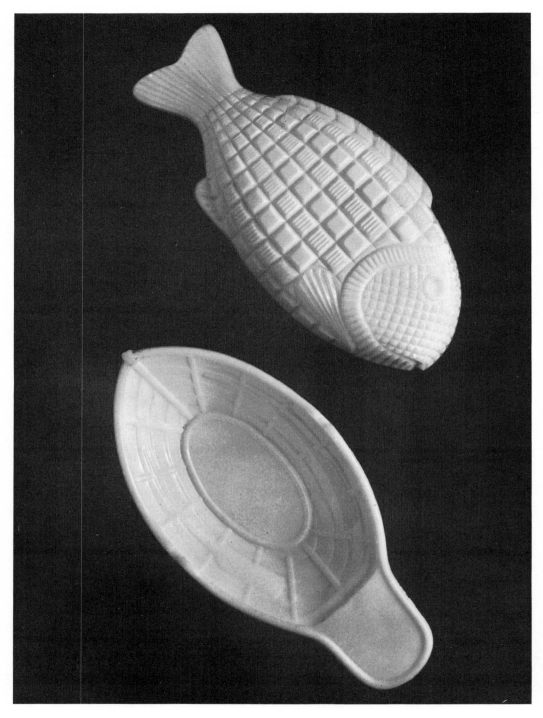

62b. *Boat Pickle Dish:* Even bears the name *Pickle* at the front end. 9½″ long, 4½″ from oar lock to oar lock. On the bottom appears *Patented Feb. 17, 1874.* 62a. *Fish Pickle Tray:* You are looking at the bottom of this tray. 9¼″ from mouth to tail tip, 4½″ through the middle, slightly opalescent in color. The design detail is well done.

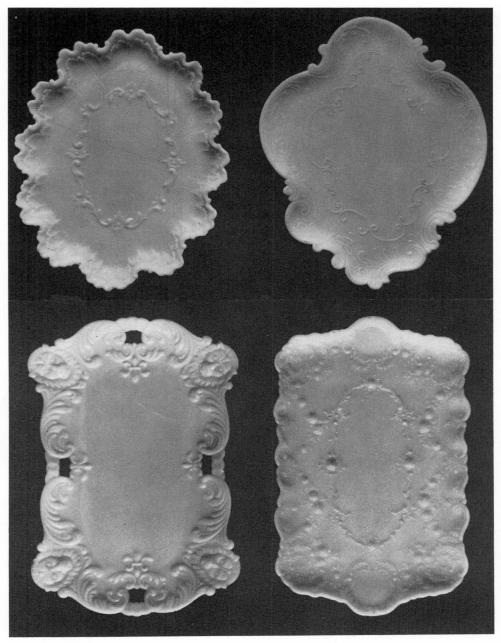

63a. *Versailles Pattern Tray:* This is a very common and comparatively recent pattern. Thousands of pieces, including everything from water pitchers to dresser sets, were produced at the turn of the century by Dithridge & Company of Pittsburgh, Pennsylvania. Size: 11″ long by 8¼″ wide. 63b. *Fine Beaded Design Dresser Tray:* Freshly washed, this dresser tray has a startling appearance: all the hundreds of small beads in the design sparkle like little iridescent pearls. The opalescence in the glass causes this illusion. This tray is 11¼″ by 9¾″ in size.

63c. *Monkey Face Tray:* Designers were running low on ideas when they produced this! They threw in scrolls, fleur de lis, and monkey faces. The tray is poor quality Milk Glass. This is just one of dozens of dresser tray patterns that flooded the market at about 1900. Size: 11″ by 6¾″. 63d. *Garland Of Roses Tray:* Ropes and chains of roses are very popular decorative motifs for dresser trays. Whenever designers run out of new ideas they apparently revert to roses. I know of at least a dozen dresser trays with a rose theme. Size is 11¼″ by 7″.

64a. *Versailles Pickle Dish:* An odd-shaped little relish or pickle dish. 9″ long by 4¾″ at
the widest point. The gilt paint covering the border had to be removed.   64b. *Wheat
Pattern Relish Dish:* This is an inside view. Bundle of ripe wheat is center design. Underside is far more ornate than top. Sixteen panels, each with a sheaf of wheat fanning out
in an oval completely around the base. Size: 4½″ by 8″.

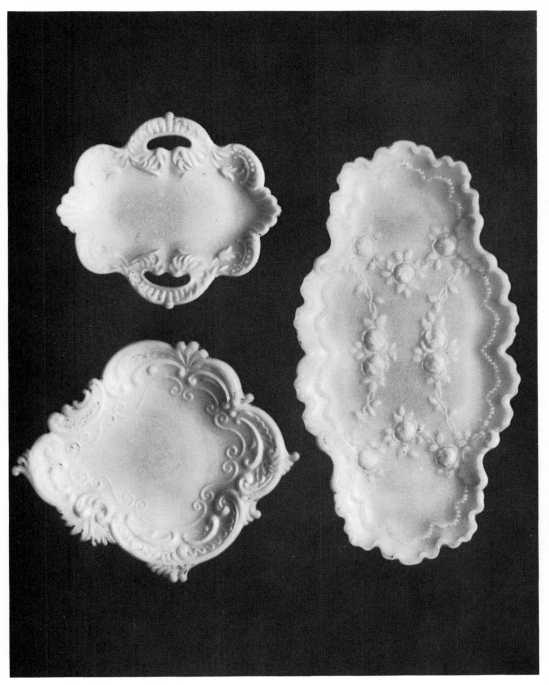

65a, b, c. *Pin Tray Assortment:* The large tray, 9¼″ by 5″, is the well known Versailles pattern in bluish white. The medium tray, 6¼″ by 5¼″, is a Scroll Variant, also in bluish white. The small tray is a marked McKee Brothers piece, 4¾″ by 4¼″, in milk white.

Chapter Four

Pitchers and Syrup Jugs

ANTIQUE MILK GLASS pitchers are about the most utilitarian antiques, all considered. The large water pitchers or smaller cream pitchers may be used about the house in many ways: on the dining-room table, as decorative pieces, or as flower containers. Pouring milk from a Milk Glass pitcher into a Milk Glass tumbler or goblet adds much to its palatability, and water poured from a Milk Glass pitcher seems to have an unusual tang and taste. Many of the larger pitchers make particularly good containers for flowers. Rather tall, they are ideal for long-stemmed roses, gladioli, chrysanthemums, and other long-stemmed beauties of the flower world. A casual decorative touch in the living room dining room, or bedroom may be achieved if the attractive designs and graceful forms of many of the pitchers are put to use.

The small creamers also lend themselves to floral decoration. Blue bachelor buttons, orange or yellow nasturtiums, or wide-eyed pansies tucked into the mouth of a Milk Glass creamer find a striking setting for their floral beauty. A friend of mine, an ardent flower-club member, tells me that she has won blue ribbons with her Milk Glass entries.

Milk Glass pitchers, both large and small, must have been extremely popular two or three generations ago, judging by the number of opaque pitchers still available to the collector. I must have between fifty and sixty choice pitchers in my own collection, assembled during the past several years.

Tall tankards like the white Scroll Water pitcher, the blue Beaded Band and Center pitcher, and the slim, high-lipped Shell Foot pattern with lavender violets painted on the side are only a few of my prizes. (These three tankard-style pitchers are from 9″ to 12½″ in height.)

Milk Glass pitchers come in an assortment of sizes and shapes almost as diversified as lamps. There are, besides the tall tankards, squat syrup pitchers, lean milk pitchers, pot-bellied jugs and stately creamers, with applied handles or with pressed handles, and with narrow lips or wide spouts. The designs range from intricate geometric patterns to beautifully executed profiles of people, and from dainty flower paintings to black and white decalcomanias.

A rather unusual milk pitcher is the Basket Weave design with the none too popular yet lifelike snake handle. It is remarkable that these snake-handled pitchers have survived, despite an almost universal loathing for snakes. I have seen people, upon recognizing the snake, involuntarily thrust the pitcher from them or drop it in pure fright!

One of the handsomest and most expertly detailed water pitchers shown in this chapter is the famous Owl design. The outstanding work of the mold-maker in designing the large Owl pitcher is clearly apparent in the two photographs included herein. With both front and side views to examine, you can note the intricate and painstaking details of the feathers, the four-leaf clovers, the cherries, and the cherry leaves. Also illustrated is one of the small Owl creamers which, on first glance, appears to be the same design as the large pitcher. In the small pitcher, however, the detail is entirely feathers and leaves; while in the large one, there are feathers, four-leaf clovers, cherries, and leaves—all discernible.

There is an unusually attractive large water pitcher, originally part of a set including tumblers. I show only the pitcher, which in the illustration deceptively appears to be speckled or spotted. Actually, this effect was caused by flecks of gold being thrown on at the last moment and melted into the glass while it was still hot. I have called this pattern *Curtain,* but I understand that it has been called by several other names. Whatever its name, this lovely pitcher has certain characteristics all its own. It is markedly different from most of American Milk Glass and has every appearance and feature of Bristol, the English glass so popular in vases. However, this pitcher is definitely American. Its stunning appearance results from its heaviness, brilliant lustre, and completeness of design.

Blue Milk Glass water pitchers are rare. Milk white is the predominating color for pitchers, both large and small. I do not recall ever having seen a color other than white in syrup jugs with the exception of Daisy pattern, which I have seen in light blue and chartreuse green in addition to white.

The Rose Sprig water pitcher in Milk Glass is outstanding. It is almost necessary to keep my own under lock and key to prevent it from disappearing. I know at least six designing collectors who have openly threatened to kidnap this pitcher if ever they find it unattended.

One of the very late patterns, a most colorful and attractive pitcher sometimes called *Windmill* (referred to by Mrs. Kamm as the "Marigold Windmill"), was produced in great quantity between 1910 and 1920 by the Imperial Glass Company. One of the imponderables in the antique world is "What *becomes* of an item produced in thousands upon thousands?" such as, for example, this Windmill pitcher. Where do they all disappear to? Were they broken and relegated to the ash heap? Are they hiding on the topmost pantry shelf or gathering dust in the attic? They certainly are not cluttering up the antique shops, and the cause certainly is not that the average antique dealer knows the tender age of this typical dodo of the glass world and refuses to handle it. It is incredible that so many can be reduced to so few in so short a time!

There are many Milk Glass syrup or molasses jugs, perhaps because syrup, molasses, and honey were used more frequently in our grandmothers' time than they are today. Note some of the ornate pewter tops on the earlier syrup jugs. There are, for example, the bird atop the Stippled Dahlia piece, the dolphin finial on the Palmette syrup jug, and the little round ball on the cover of the stubby little jug with the painted design.

You will find most of the early Milk Glass syrup jugs with applied handles sporting peaked pewter tops, while those of later vintage without applied handles seem able to afford only a cheap tinny metal cover.

One of the rarest syrups shown is the very early Bell Flower design. This pattern has long been eagerly sought after by collectors of clear pressed glass. To unearth one in white Milk Glass is to find a real treasure.

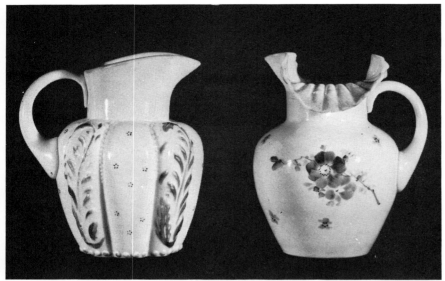

66b. *Wild Rose Design Pitcher*
The two flowered pitchers shown
here have no early ancestry, n
famous pattern name. They a
simply a pair of run-of-the-mi
white Milk Glass water pitcher
The Wild Rose Design on th
ruffled top pitcher is beautifull
executed, making this piece a d
lightful decorative piece f
everyday use. 66a. *Floral Dec*
rated Pitcher: Bolder than th
Wild Rose both in color and i
shape, this piece is less attractiv
yet serviceable.

66c. *Syrup Jug with Pewter Bir*
Top: This is just a severely plai
milk white syrup jug, whos
handle is crudely applied an
whose pewter top is adorned b
a quaintly designed pewter bir
There is no pattern, no frills, n
over-all design on the Milk Glas
body of the jug. This is definitel
an early piece, and its strict sin
plicity gives it unusual charn

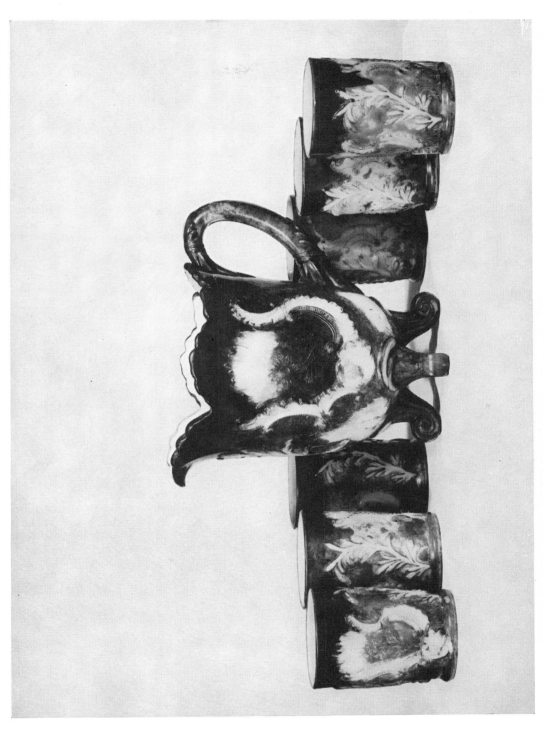

67. *Blue Decorated Pitchers and Tumblers:* A heavy set—heavy in weight and deep in color, the latter having been painted on with great gusto. This set is an excellent example of a Milk Glass disguise so effective that its own manufacturer would hardly recognize his product but for the fact that the inside of each piece was left untouched by paint.

68. *Bryan Milk Glass Pitcher:* This interesting pitcher, which shows the bust of William Jennings Bryan on its side, is identical with the Wild Rose Design Pitcher, Illus. 114, even to the wild rose design. There is no doubt that these two pitchers were produced at the same factory, and that the wild flower paintings are the work of one artist. The bust of Bryan looks like a decalcomania of some kind, which, rarely applied to a pitcher, are often found on plates.

69. *Dolphin Pitchers:* Classifying these two Dolphin covered pieces is a problem. The bases of these have handles and spouts, so I place them among the pitcher group. They are an attractive pair, however classified; the detail on cover and base is excellent, and the pieces difficult to obtain in pairs. *From the I. M. Wiese Collection, Silver Mine, Connecticut.*

70a, b, c. *Pewter Topped Syrup Jugs*: Syrup jugs are legion. In my wanderings I have seen hundreds; those selected for this book are handles and pewter tops. The patterns shown are called, respectively, Panel, Beehive, and Curtain. These pieces vary slightly in

71. *Blue Rain Drop Water Pitcher:* Large blue Milk Glass water pitcher with a rim of whitish opalescence around top and bottom, this pattern looks similar to *Thousand Eye* but definitely is not. A colorful piece, excellent for decoration, the pitcher is 7½″ high and 4½″ across the base; it comes in blue only.

72. *Paneled Leaf Creamer:* A very early cream pitcher in milk white, the Paneled Leaf has a most intriguing applied handle. The pattern is so unique that I have found it on no other piece such as sugar, butter, compote, etc. Size: 5¾″ in height, 2⅞″ in base width.

73a, b, c. *Palmette, Rose Leaf, and Hobnail Syrup Jugs:* Excellent examples of pewter-topped applied handle syrups: Palmette is a well-known pressed glass pattern; Rose Leaf is a design frequently found as a decoration of Milk Glass pieces; and Hobnail needs little commentary for the experienced collector. All three are approximately the same height. A slightly different belly contour gives each pitcher its own personality.

74a. *Gooseberry Creamer:* A small opalescent Milk Glass creamer similar to other Milk Glass berry patterns such as Strawberry and Blackberry. The detail of the berries and leaves is good. A beaded band goes completely around the pitcher, above and below the center motif of leaves and fruit. 4¼″ tall and 3″ across the base, white only. 74b, c. *Tree of Life and Beaded Heart Jugs:* White Milk Glass. Of later date, these have tinny tops and molded handles. The Tree of Life Jug, fairly common, comes in blue, green, and white. The more scarce Beaded Heart Jug appears in white only.

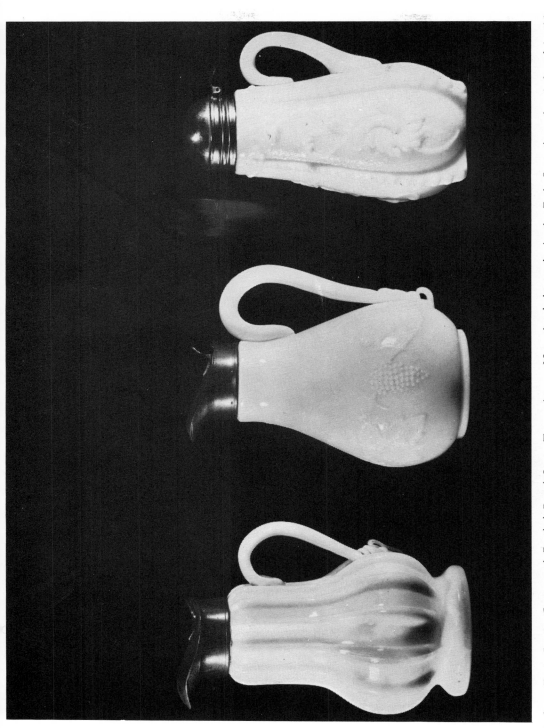

75a, b, c. *Early Loop, Grape and Beaded Panel Jugs:* Two aristocrats and a commoner stand side by side in this grouping: two pewter-topped, one metalized; two applied handles, one molded. Note the dark streaks in the Early Loop jug, always found in this pattern, whether compote, covered sugar, or syrup. B is a conventional Grape and Leaf pattern; C is a late pitcher of the paint era.

76a, b, c. *Painted Leaf, Chain and Fan, Rose Jugs:* Three more milk white syrups of varying shapes. Except for attractive design, there are no outstanding features.

77. *Bell Flower Syrup Jug:* Early Bell Flower, this is a narrow ribbed syrup with applied handle and pewter top. A collectors' piece, it is rare and most desirable, for seldom does one find Bell Flower in Milk Glass. I have seen several syrup jugs and an open salt dish in this pattern of Milk Glass. Bell Flower is one of the earliest pressed glass patterns. *From the Lucian Clark Bareham Collection, Mercersburg, Pennsylvania.*

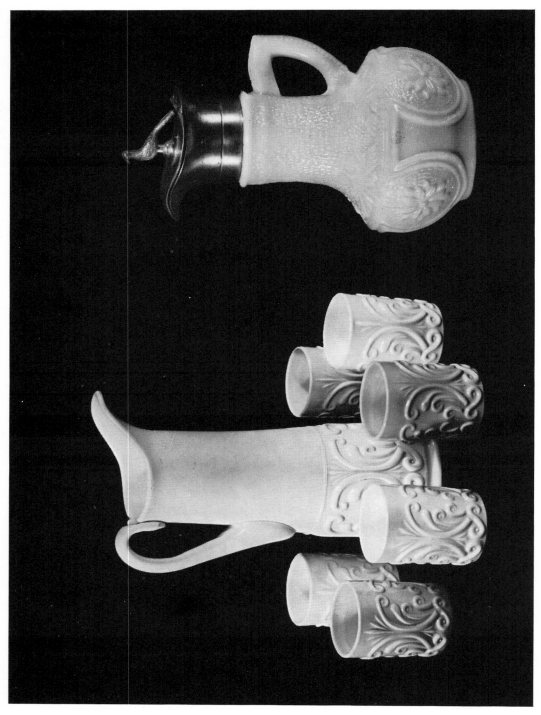

78a. *Scroll Tankard and Tumblers:* A very popular pattern, manufactured in considerable quantity. The tankard appears in white and blue, the tumblers in white, blue, and occasionally in chartreuse green. They are 3¾″ tall.

78b. *Stippled Dahlia Syrup Jug:* Atop the jug is a beautiful bird, exquisitely executed in pewter. The jug is of usual height, milk white. *From the collection of Mrs. Harry Bell, Seattle, Washington.*

79. *Curtain Pattern Gold Flecked Pitcher:* This strikingly beautiful pitcher must be seen to be appreciated. Its unusually clear pattern detail would make it an outstanding piece, but the added feature of small flakes of gold applied to the surface before the glass cooled makes the pitcher extraordinarily intriguing. This rare piece is part of a complete set consisting originally of six tumblers and the pitcher. The pieces of this set are heavy, fine examples of the work of Milk Glass craftsmen.

80. *Owl Pitcher—Front View:* This is a closeup of the popular Owl Milk Glass Pitcher, large size. The Owl Pattern comes in three sizes of pitchers: large, medium, and small. The feathers are expertly detailed, as can be seen easily in this front view photograph. The small pitcher in this Owl Pattern is sometimes found in blue. The large glass eyes give this old fellow a truly owlish look. *From the collection of Mrs. Dale Myers, Howe, Indiana.*

81. *Owl Pitcher—Side View:* The side view of the large Owl Milk Glass Pitcher shows more detail than the front view. Note the four-leaf clovers, the cherries, and the cherry leaves, in addition to the bird's feathers. I have recently examined a small blue Owl Pitcher that greatly resembles this pitcher except for the side decorations. This small pitcher has an all-feather motif; no four-leaf clovers, cherries, or leaves. *From the collection of Mrs. Dale Myers, Howe, Indiana.*

82b, c. *Sunflower Creamer and Open Sugar Bowl:* Most of the pieces in this pattern are of a beautiful chalk white. 82a. *Swan Creamer:* Snow white, 4¾″ across the top from tip of spout to handle edge, 5″ tall.

83. *Cosmos Water Pitcher:* An excellent likeness of the well known Cosmos Pattern, this is a large pitcher, two quarts in capacity. The charm of the pastel coloring of the flowers—blue, pink, and yellow—placed over the netting design background, makes Cosmos a truly desirable pattern. No pitcher collection is complete without a Cosmos item, creamer, milk pitcher, or large water pitcher, in its midst. The wide band of the neck in this particular pitcher is pink; I have seen necks also in blue, yellow and gray. The piece is 9″ tall and 6½″ across the middle.

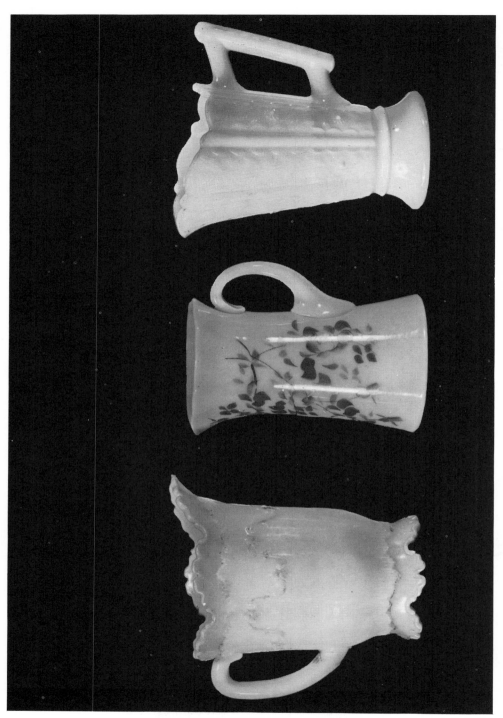

84a, b. *Versailles* and *Conventional Water Pitchers:* Not an overly attractive pattern, Versailles is late and fairly plentiful; produced by Dithridge & Co. around 1900. The other pitcher is plain Milk Glass, with painted Leaf and Flower. The heavy Milk Glass in this pitcher is good quality. 84c. *Paneled Daisy Creamer:* 5½" from base to tip of pouring spout; 3" across base; and 5½" from tip of spout to top of handles.

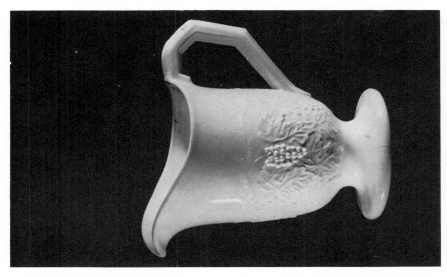

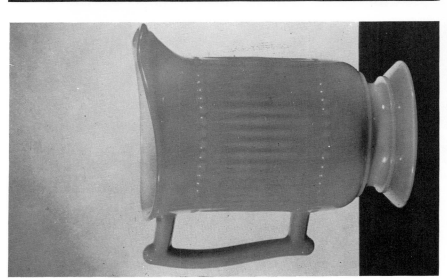

85a. *Blue Dart Bar Water Pitcher:* A very light blue water pitcher in the Dart Bar Pattern. In fact, this is a distinctly different light blue from most blue Milk Glass. The edges of this piece border on opalescence; the dimensions are 8″ in height, 4½″ in base width, and 5″ in width across the top from side to side. The pattern is found more often in white, and tumblers are rarely found in blue. *85b. Square Block Pitcher:* This is a late piece, so late it can scarcely claim an antique heritage, but sufficiently good looking to be seen in numerous antique shops and occasionally in Milk Glass collections. It is being reproduced today by Westmoreland, which calls it Pattern No. 500. 85c. *Grape Pattern Creamer:* A chalky white Milk Glass creamer, about 5½″ high and approximately 3″ across the base. There are many grape patterns and designs in Milk Glass. The details of grapes and grape leaves on this creamer are well molded.

86. *Rose Sprig Milk Pitcher:* One of the loveliest Milk Glass pitchers I have seen, this design incorporates a lovely open rose on a stem with leaves centered in the middle of a beaded panel on each side of the snow white pitcher. This is Milk Glass at its best: proud, dainty, usable. In size is 7¾″ tall with a 3¾″ base; 4¼″ across the scalloped top.

87. (*Marigold*) *Windmill Water Pitcher:* Three oval panels surround this large Milk Glass pitcher. The two side panels are identical, each showing a windmill scene with trees and split rail fences. The front oval features a man fishing from a boat, trees, more split rail fences, and a charming lake shore cottage. This is an extremely heavy pitcher; a limb of a tree forms its handle. The precision and quantity of work that went into the design of this pitcher makes the piece stand out as one of the most finely decorated Milk Glass items. 8½″ in height and 5″ in width across the middle, this is a product of the Imperial Glass Company, who produced the Windmill Pitcher in great quantity in the 1910 decade.

88. *Geometric Three-Mold Water Pitcher:* An extremely rare Geometric Pattern pitcher in blown glass, this piece is 7″ tall and 5″ wide at the center. The pattern is rare in clear glass, and certainly rare in milk white. This particular Milk Glass pitcher comes in white only, with an applied handle. It is a piece worthy to associate with the finest Milk Glass.

89. *Oval Daisy Pattern Pitcher:* Tall and stately with a schoolgirl figure, this example is Milk Glass at its best, for purely decorative use. When I first found the piece, it was heavily decorated in green, pink, and red. Garish was the word for it, but with the rouge removed you see the lovely piece above. Size: 10″ tall, with a narrow 4″ base.

90a. *Beaded Circle Variant:* The tall tankard seen here is light blue, and Millard refers to it as the *Beaded Circle Pattern*. It is definitely a variant of the Beaded Circle Design, but I have never been able to unearth its true name. It is 9¾″ tall and 4¼″ across the base, and found in blue only. 90b. *Swirl Creamer:* The small Swirl Creamer is one of the many Swirl Pattern pieces. Mrs. Kamm shows at least a half dozen in her Pitcher Books and this one doesn't exactly match any of them. This creamer is blue, of good heavy glass, and probably was made for the premium trade.

91a. *Primrose Creamer:* Of the 1880 period. *Oval:* 9″ tall, 5½″ diameter, 4″ across base. 91b. *Owl Miniature Creamer:* 3½″ in height 91c. *Basket Weave with Snake:* Snake handle. and 2″ across the base. 91d. *Diamonds in* 7″ high, 5½″ across the middle, 4¼″ base.

92. *Marquis and Marchioness Creamer:* This creamer is so English it fairly shouts its ancestry. Beautifully executed in design detail, it portrays a likeness of both the Marquis and the Marchioness of Lorne on opposite sides of the pitcher. The date is 1878, celebrating the arrival of the royal pair in Nova Scotia on November 25 of that year. The beaded work of the ovals, which extend around the top and in bands about the base, is most outstanding. I know of few handsomer creamers in Milk Glass. This piece was found in Canada and its owner claimed her grandmother had "fetched it over" from the old country.

93a, c. *Rose Jars:* These Rose Jars are a pair except for color. The one on the left is white, and the other blue with a blue cover darker than the base. No great rarities. 93b. *Ribbed Shell Creamer:* A jug with- out its top, this is a beautiful blue piece. The rough rim indicates a missing metal top. Millard, however, refers to this piece as a creamer, and I follow.

94. *Little Boy Pitcher:* This is a rare Milk Glass item. I have seen it in a sugar and a spooner as well as in the cream pitcher shown. The detail, especially of the flowers around the head, is excellent and the quality of the glass is the best.

95a. *Shell-Footed Water Pitcher:* One of the tallest of the Milk Glass tankard-style pitchers, this has little feet instead of the usual flat base. The painting on the side of this pitcher, although crude, is smart-looking with its blue violets and green leaves. 95b. *Hinge Shaving Mug:* Be-cause of its design and pattern, I think it best to include the shaving mug in this chapter. I call the pattern *Hinge* because of its hinge-like design on sides and back. 95c. *Star Creamer:* A four-pointed star on either side of this creamer gives it its name. Heavy milk white Milk Glass.

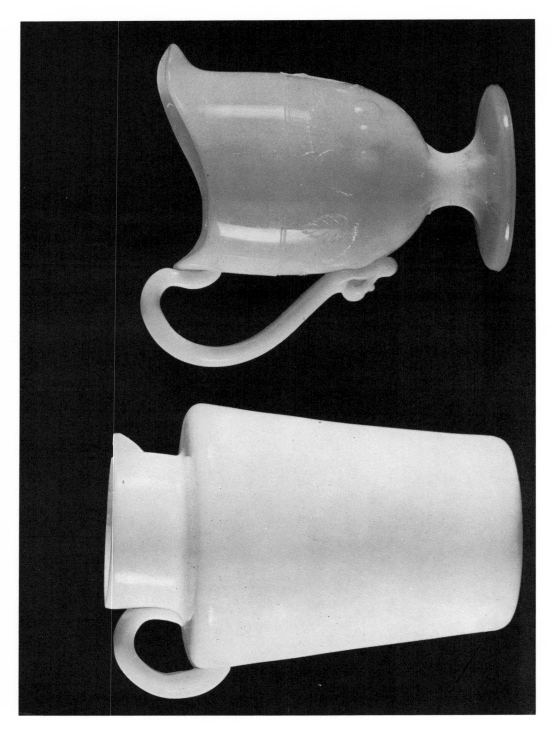

96b. *Cherry Creamer:* Design is very indistinct. The main body of the creamer has a marked bluish watered milk color, while the handle is snow white. 3″ across the base and 5¼″ high. 96a. *Just Plain Jug:* The rough top ridge of this jug indicates that it should have a pewter or metal top. No pattern, no design, 4″ at its widest point and 5½″ tall.

97a. *Daisy and Tree-Limb Pitcher:* A water pitcher, only 7″ tall with a 4½″ base. *From the Van Doran Collection, Clinton, Michigan.*

97b. *Shell Pitcher:* The pattern causes considerable confusion because it does not have the shell feet usually associated with the Shell Foot Pattern.

98. *Jersey Glass Pitcher:* Reported to be a product of The Jersey Glass Company of Jersey City, N. J., c. 1825–1850, this beautiful blown hand-wrought piece is the earliest piece of Milk Glass shown in this book and probably one of the earliest and rarest pieces in existence. *Courtesy Metropolitan Museum of Art, New York.*

Chapter Five

Bowls and Compotes

BOWLS AND COMPOTES, open and covered, with or without standards, offer a wide variety for the Milk Glass collector. The choice of patterns is considerably limited, however, when compared with the great assortment of patterns in clear pressed glass. The latter number well over a thousand, whereas there are only a few hundred in Milk Glass. It is true that many well-known pressed-glass patterns may be found also in Milk Glass.

Complete sets for table use, including bowls and compotes, sugars and creamers, and pitchers and tumblers, are both limited and rare in Milk Glass. There are a number of patterns collectible in Milk Glass sets nevertheless. The most common of these are: Strawberry, Sawtooth, Blackberry (reproduced), Wheat, Cherry, Grape, Princess Feather, Gooseberry, Waffle, Icicle, Melon, Roman Cross, Crossed Fern, Daisy, Scroll, Tree of Life, Basket Weave, Corn (Maise), Cosmos, Beaded Jewel (reproduced), Block and Fan, Sunflower, Paneled Daisy, Stippled Forget-Me-Not, Shell Pattern, Swan, Swan and Cattails (reproduced), Barred Hobnail, Cameo, Teardrop and Tassel, Versailles.

In addition to these, collectors will occasionally find a piece of Milk Glass in one of the better-known, early clear pressed glass patterns. These are seldom found, and I doubt that they were ever manufactured in complete sets or in any sizable quantity. Examples of these rarities are: † Liberty Bell, large platter; † Hamilton with Leaf, low covered compote; † Bell Flower, syrup jug; Hobnail, both bowl and tumbler; † Thousand Eye, bowl; † Thumbprint, bowl and saucers; † Almond Thumbprint, sugar bowl; Classic water pitcher; † Daisy Swirl, covered sugar bowl; Tulip, covered butter dish; † Daisy and Button, both bowl and pickle dish; † Buckle, bowl; † Loop, large compote and covered sugar and finally, Jacob's Coat, covered butter dish.

The large group of open-edge or lacy-edge bowls and compotes offer interesting items for collection. There are many fine specimens shown throughout this chapter.

There are some intriguing bowls in Milk Glass that open new fields of discovery and exploration—bowls whose designs and workmanship arouse the enthusiasm of glass collectors everywhere. Not too much is known about many of the smaller factories of the Pittsburgh, Wheeling, Ohio, and Indiana areas where these bowls and compotes were manufactured. Nor can credit be attributed to the specific creator of the designs. Some of the best examples of these bowls are the Swirl bowl, the imitation cut glass bowl, the low Lacy-Edge bowls, and the handpainted Tree of Life bowl. Each has its own interesting personality, charm of contour, and detail of design.

The works of the larger and better-known factories, such as Challinor, Taylor and Company of Tarentum, Pennsylvania, the Atter-

† Illustrated in this book.

bury Company of Pittsburgh, Pennsylvania, and the Richards and Hartley Company, also of Tarentum, have been shown and written about frequently before this. In fact, the experienced collector can almost tell an Atterbury or Challinor, Taylor product on sight. Many of the pieces in this chapter, however, were created by the numerous smaller Milk Glass factories throughout the country.

The predominating color found in bowls and compotes is milk white. Now and then a blue one comes to light or a rare green specimen appears from nowhere. As far as I have been able to discover, there are no antique black Milk Glass bowls or compotes, with the exception of a Ram's Head bowl— the only early black bowl I know of. If you find any black or deep amethyst examples, they are not old. I have seen a few but their history did not date before the 1920's. There were, of course, pieces in purple or caramel slag, and quite a few in custard glass. In passing, too, I must mention the truly rare lavender Ram's Head bowl which we reproduce here in color.

99. *Scroll Round Bowl:* Another example of the well-known Scroll pattern. A round low bowl without standard. This same size bowl also is mounted on a 4½" base. Measurements are 8¼" across from edge to edge and 3½" deep. It may be found in several Milk Glass colors: milk white, blue and chartreuse green. The quality of the glass is excellent and the beautiful Scroll design covers the bottom of the bowl as well as the sides.

100a. *Arch Border Bowl:* Milk white, made by Atterbury in the 1880's. Also comes in blue. It measures 8″ across. Every time I find a piece of Arch Border design and consider its fragile border I marvel at its length of life. *100b. *Ball and Chain Edge Bowl:* Bluish white with a fiery opalescent edge. 3¼″ deep and 8″ in diameter. One of the rarer patterns. An attractive flower, like a small forget-me-not, in the center of each circle. Its frilly open-edge work somewhat re-sembles the Arch pattern of Atterbury. West-moreland's reproduction has a very marked flare to the border.   100c. *Lattice-Edge Open Bowl:* Approximately 3″ deep by 8″ across. Made by Atterbury. These lovely bowls often had the same hand-painted center decorations as the Lattice-Edge plates. This one has an apple blossom decoration. They can be found in milk white and rarely in blue.

101. *Pair of Tree of Life Painted Bowls:* This stunning pair of Tree of Life covered bowls may be found either painted or plain. Their manufacture is attributed to the Portland Glass Company. The painting on these bowls varies greatly, from bright vivid colors to faded washed out affairs which probably resulted from too many in-dustrious washings by some owners. The less washing and cleaning a painted Milk Glass piece undergoes, the longer it will retain its original colors. *From the collection of Mrs. William Bullock, Toledo, Ohio.*

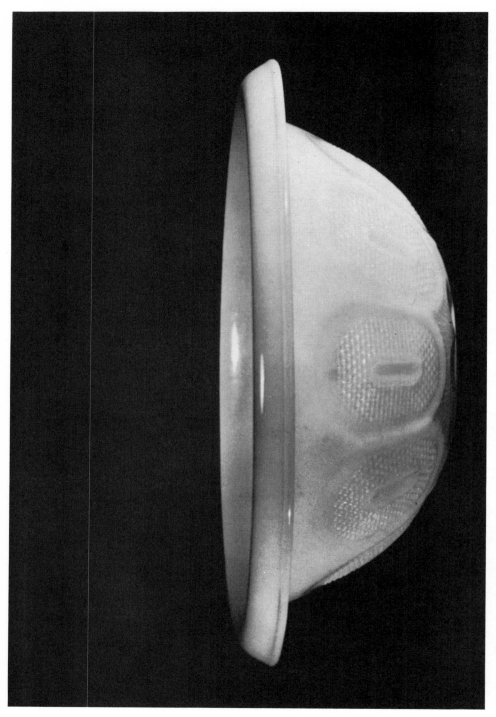

102. *Buckle Bowl M.G.:* This beautiful fiery opalescent Buckle pattern bowl, measuring 10″ across by 3¼″ deep, is a great rarity and was undoubtedly produced at Sandwich. That the Buckle is definitely a Sandwich pattern is proved by fragments preserved at M.I.T. This piece is very heavy and follows the distinctive opalescence of other early Sandwich Milk Glass pieces. A piece of really early Sandwich Milk Glass is clearly different from that produced by any other factory because of its outstanding and distinctive beauty of color.

103. *Atlas Scalloped Compote:* Here is our friend Atlas (or Hercules). Same little fellow as shown on next page only with a plain scalloped edge bowl atop his bent shoulders instead of a Lacy-Edge bowl. Both this and the next piece are Atterbury products and show their usual excellent design and workmanship. This plain scalloped top is the more common of the two types. But both are tops in the Milk Glass field and are definitely collectors' pieces.

104. *Atlas Open-Edge Compote:* Poor little Atlas, if such be his correct name, standing all these years supporting a sizable 8¼ inch open bowl atop his bent shoulders. This unusual piece is sometimes called Gnome or Hercules, but Atlas seems to be the more popular name. This piece comes both with open-edged top as shown here or with scalloped top as shown on preceding page. Both pieces are attributed to Atterbury. Height, 8¼ inches. Color, milk white. *From the collection of Mrs. Dale Myers, Howe, Ind.*

105. *Acanthus Leaf Bowl:* A really charming bowl that resembles an opening flower. Very heavy in good quality milk white glass, measuring approximately 10″ across and nearly 5″ in depth. The leaf decoration around the exterior is beautifully executed. Even on the bottom, where it cannot be seen unless turned bottom up, there is still another interesting leaf decoration. The large petal effect, three in number, is a most unusual border treatment. The maker of this stunning bowl is unknown to the author.

106a. *Daisy and Button:* An extremely heavy bowl with a very deeply cut design. 3¼″ deep by 9¼″ across the top. There is a rim inside the bowl evidently for a top or cover. Yet none of the bowls in this pattern that I have seen had covers.   106b. *Lattice-Edge Closed Bowl:* Made by Atterbury in blue and in milk white. Very popular with hand-painted centers of flowers— this one has a trumpet vine painting—conven-tional designs, and occasionally a bird motif. 106c. *Hexagon Daisy and Tree of Life Bowl:* This bowl is a hybrid. The surface is divided into six panels. Three contain the Tree of Life pattern and the other three contain a Daisy pattern. The inside of the bowl is ribbed and on the inside bottom is a Daisy design. It is 8¼″ at the top and approximately 4″ deep.

107. *Corn or Maize Pattern:* This interesting Corn pattern was manufactured by the W. L. Libby & Son Company of Toledo, Ohio and called "Maize Art Glass." Mrs. Kamm shows an interesting trade journal advertisement of this product, dated August 1, 1889, on Plate 22 in her *Fifth Pitcher Book.* It is a good looking pattern with its green hand-painted husks contrasting with the milk white background. This is not a rare pattern. In the Midwest many such pieces may be found. The piece shown with the bowl is a celery. 8½" across by 3½" deep.

108a. *Wide Weave Basket Bowl:* A small heavy bowl, only 3¼″ deep and a mere 8″ across. Another bowl with the appearance of ironstone china. The basket weave design is very different from the conventional basket design found on so many Milk Glass pieces. Evidently an early bowl and rare. 108b. *King's Crown Bowl:* This is an interesting Milk Glass bowl with eight points of the crown forming the border. The predominat-ing pattern seems to be a narrow basket weave completely around the bowl. Height, 3¾″, and approximately 8″ across. Fairly good glass and a reasonably rare piece. 108c. *Wide Ribbed Bowl: 1870* is heavily imprinted on the base of this sturdy bowl. Very heavy and rings like a fire gong when tapped. At first glance it looks like a piece of heavy ironstone china. It measures 4″ high and 9¼″ rim to rim at the top.

109a. *Thousand Eye Bowl:* Light blue and milk white. 4½″ deep with an 8″ diameter. Richard and Hartlet, accredited creators. Splendid glass.

Rare. 109b. *Thumb Print Bowl:* Attributed to Bakewell, Pears and Co. Very rare. Glass is beautiful chalk white. 8″ across and 3″ deep.

110a. *Waffle Pattern Bowl:*
smart pattern and an early o
Very heavy and made of exc
lent quality Milk Glass. This
a large bowl, approximately
across the top and a good 41
tall without its cover. It origina
had a cover which was lost ma
years before I added this pie
to my collection. Waffle is
popular collector's pattern a
still may be found in a set. 11(
Daisy Pattern Bowl: The Da
pattern pieces came in varic
colors of Milk Glass. I have se
cruets in green, blue, white a
one variety of pink. This Da
bowl comes in white and bl
The milk white pieces were oft
brilliantly hand-painted. T
bowls are frequently found wi
a plain scalloped edge, rath
than the open fancy work of th
piece. The Daisy bowls are c
lightful examples of Milk Gl
and always bring good pric

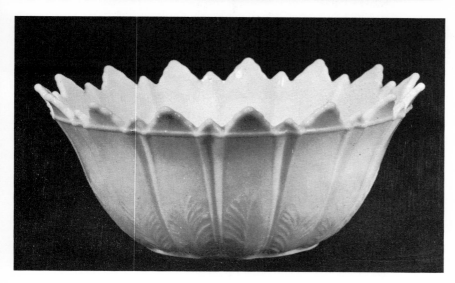

110c. *Acanthus Leaf Bowl:* F
many years I was unable to fi
this pattern, and then, in l
than six months, I must ha
stumbled over fifty in my trave
I have one in purple slag, o
in milk white and one in lig
blue clear pressed glass. I belie
it was Ruth Lee who said, "O
way to tell really old white Mi
Glass is to look for the oyste
in the glass." This piece has
many oysters (one in each of
fourteen panels) that I start
looking for the pearls. It is
fairly deep bowl, 4½", and 1(
across.

111. *Basket Weave Compote:* An open compote that should have a cover. I have seen this compote with the wrong cover several times but only once with the correct one. It was in an antique dealer's window and the sign on her front door read, "Gone to Rochester, back tomorrow." Tomorrow I was five hundred miles away. Size, nearly 7½″ tall with an 8″ diameter. A patent mark on the bottom on the base, *Pat'd June 30. '74.*

112a. *"S" Bowl:* A rare and unusual treatment of the "S" pattern. I marvel that a bowl with such a fragile border could pass down through the years unscathed. It is small, only 7¼" across the top and 2¼" deep. 112b. *Spaced Rib Bowl:* This slender bowl or bread tray is a rare item in Milk Glass. I have a companion bowl in a most unusual shade of green. A close inspection shows identical mold markings on both speci- mens. It is the longest (a full 13") and narrow- est (6¼") Milk Glass bowl I know of. A very delicate cabling follows the entire scalloped edge. 112c. *Long Ribbed Bowl:* Has a fluted pattern with a cable edging around the top. A beautiful wild rose hand-painted design covers the inside. 12½" long and only 3" deep. Top quality Milk Glass.

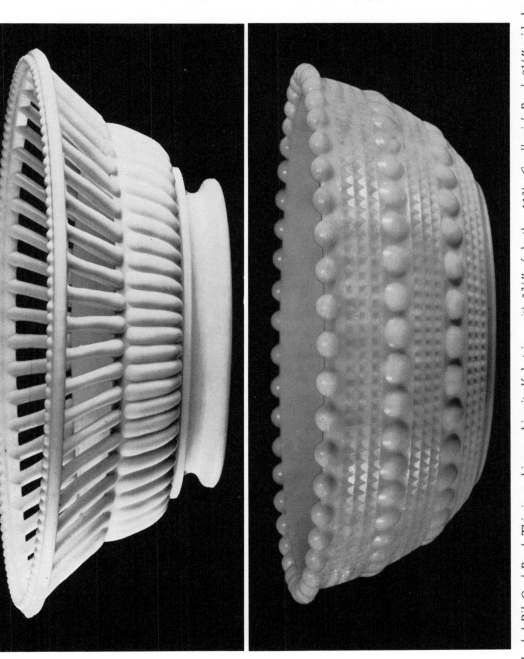

113a. *Beaded Rib Oval Bowl:* This is as china as china itself, but is actually Milk Glass. The oval is 10″ end to end and 7¼″ at center, with 3¾″ of depth. 113b. *Candlewick Bowl:* 9¼″ wide by 3½″ deep. Good glass, fair bell tone.

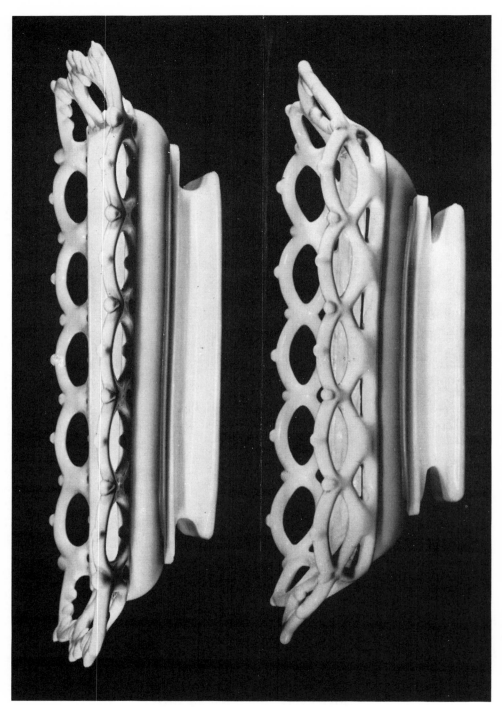

114a. *Chain-Edge Dish, Large:* This is a large Milk Glass dish, fully 13″ long, 8½″ across and approximately 3″ deep. Its chain border, however, takes up a goodly amount of space so its carrying capacity is not what it appears to be at first glance. It has a very china-like finish which one often finds in the Atterbury Company pieces. 114b.

Chain-Edge Dish, Medium. This is a smaller edition of the Chain-Edge dish. It measures only 11″ long by 7¼″ wide. It is almost identical in pattern, chain loop for chain loop. It has the usual beauty and grace of all Atterbury products.

115a. *Jeweled Medallion Bowl:* The fine deep cutting in the design of this bowl makes it look like a piece of cut glass. The designer or craftsman who made this mold must have spent much time and loving care at his job. Never have I seen more intricate detail. 8¼″ wide with a 3½″ depth. 115b. *Swirl Bowl:* The flare top of this bowl has more style than a Paris gown, while the swirl pattern shows every curve to advantage. It is a full 9½″ across the top and 4″ deep. I know of only one other piece in this particular swirl pattern, another bowl. Do not confuse the Swirl candlesticks and the Swirl pitchers with this pattern.

116a. *Wild Iris Bowl:* On this bowl gilt is splashed around on the Iris blossoms and leaves. It is 9¼" across and approximately 3" deep. This pattern is fairly common but the iris is usually painted lavender and the leaves or fronds green. The gold treatment is unusual. It is rather recent and readily found. 116b. *Fan Variant Bowl:* This is the heaviest and thickest piece of Milk Glass I know of. The glass has a slightly bluish cast to it and the mold cuts are rather deep. It is a full 10" across the top and 4¼" deep. Definitely an American piece, yet the appearance of the glass is French. Relatively rare.

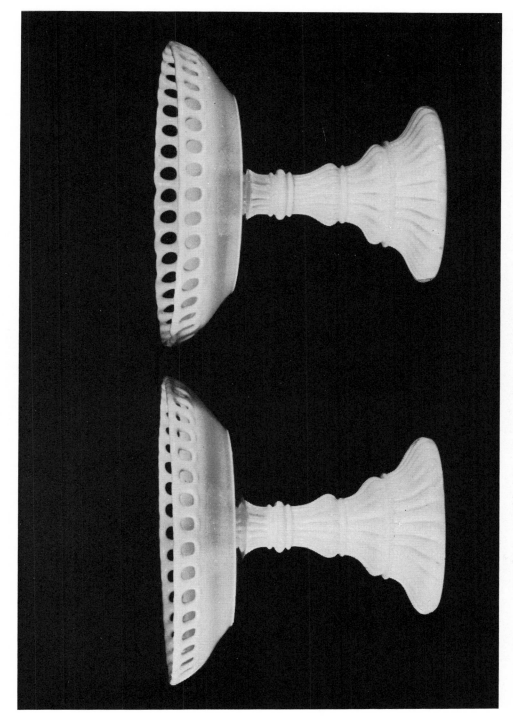

117. *Narrow Ribbed Stem Compote:* This is a less attractive piece than the Deep Ribbed Stem Compote. The bowl is much more shallow than that of the other. Height, 7″, diameter, 8¼″, depth of bowl, 2″.

118. *Deep Ribbed Stem Compote:* This picture gives a sufficiently excellent view of the detail to indicate the source of the name of this piece. It is tall, 9″, with an 8″ diameter across the top of the bowl. The bowl is 3″ deep. The open-edge design is rather crude compared with the Ribbed Stem base, which deserves a handsomer top.

*119. *Tall Ribbed Compote: No. 3 Covered Compote* is the designation given to this lovely piece by Westmoreland. in a current circular. The piece shown here is not a recent Westmoreland reproduction. I acquired it for my collection a number of years ago. If my memory is correct, I noticed this piece for the first time about 1925. I have not been able to find out whether or not Westmoreland was producing it during that period. It is now being reproduced at the Westmoreland factory and sold through department stores and gift shops. It is a beautiful Milk Glass compote either in the new or the old.

120. *Strawberry Covered Compote:* A large covered compote in the well-known strawberry pattern. I wanted to show a covered butter in the same pattern, but it was decreed otherwise. The butter was smashed into a thousand pieces in transit from Cortland Antiques Show. The compote is 8½" tall from the base to the tip of its strawberry finial and 8¼" across its plump middle.

121. *Blackberry Covered Compote:* Blackberry is a very popular Milk Glass pattern, and those who own original pieces are fortunate indeed. Some of the pieces have been reproduced, especially the goblets and the water pitcher. The reproduction is a poor copy, scarcely re-sembling the original. This picture is a good likeness of the early pattern, so examine it closely for detail. 9″ tall to the top of the large blackberry knob, 8½″ across the cover which fits over the bowl of the base.

122. *Jenny Lind Compote:* This is the famous Jenny Lind Compote. Famous because of its rarity and the fact that the base is supposed to represent the bust of Jenny Lind. Jenny should have sued the manufacturer for gross insult, libel or at least false representation. I understand Jenny Lind was a famous beauty with a charming personality. Here she is downright homely. Nevertheless, this is a rare piece of Milk Glass and brings fancy prices in the antique shops. *From the collection of Mrs. Mae Curtiss. Adrian, Michigan.*

123. *Hamilton Covered Compote:* Feast your eyes upon this rarity of rarities. I know of no other piece of Milk Glass in this early pressed glass pattern. This is the Hamilton-with-Leaf pattern, featuring a row of ivy leaves around the top of the cover and another row under the bowl. Note the pear finial atop the cover, the same as those on Hamilton covered pieces in pressed glass.

124. *Loop Sandwich Compote:* Loop is an early pressed glass pattern, rare in clear glass, extremely rare in Milk Glass. It has that odd shading of touches of black, like shadows, running through it. This pattern in Milk Glass is attributed to Sandwich where, I firmly believe, it was produced. It was made in two pieces, bowl and base, which were then joined together. It rings like a church bell when tapped and fairly exudes its early heritage.

125. *Lacy-Edge Ribbed Base Compote:* A tall and stately compote with a beautiful Lacy-Edge bowl atop a straight ribbed base. One of the tallest of Milk Glass compotes. Size (approximate), 10″ tall by 8″ across the bowl. Milk white and excellent quality glass. *From the collection of Mrs. William Bullock, Toledo, Ohio.*

126. *Open Hand Compote:* A rather different piece, eagerly sought after by collectors interested in Victorian hand pieces. The milk white bowl is absolutely plain on the outside. The cover rim around its outer edge gives evidence to a cover at one time, but I have never seen one with a cover. The bowl is nearly 10″ across. The hand grasping the column support to the bowl is artistically designed. The base is ribbed. The over-all height is 8¼″.

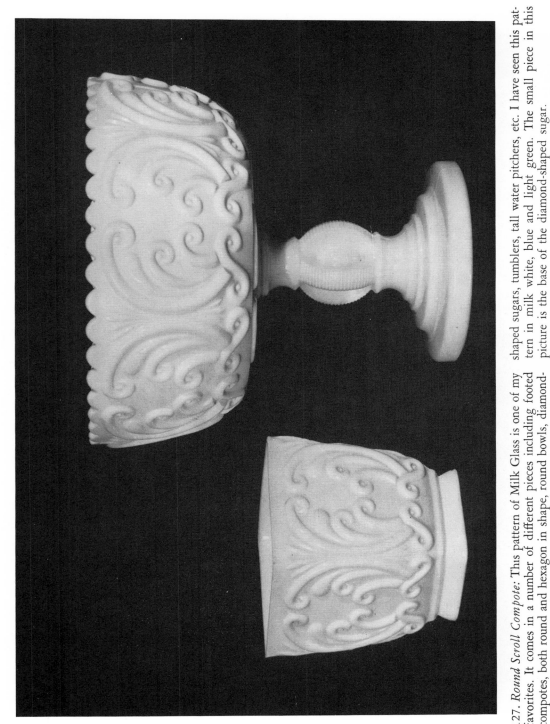

127. *Round Scroll Compote:* This pattern of Milk Glass is one of my favorites. It comes in a number of different pieces including footed compotes, both round and hexagon in shape, round bowls, diamond- shaped sugars, tumblers, tall water pitchers, etc. I have seen this pattern in milk white, blue and light green. The small piece in this picture is the base of the diamond-shaped sugar.

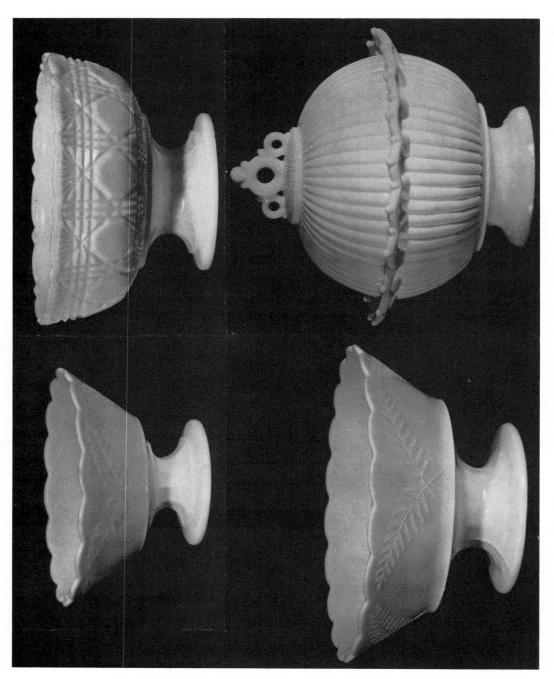

128a, c. *Crossed Fern Compotes:* 4″ tall by 8¼″ across the bowl. Do not confuse this Crossed Fern pattern with Crossed Fern and Claw and Ball pattern. 128b. *Block and Fan Bowl:* 5″ high by 8¼″ in diameter. Glass is good quality. Not too hard to find. 128d. *Covered Ribbed Bowl:* Possibly a Westmoreland creation since Westmoreland has used this pattern for other pieces.

129a. *Dutch Windmill Bowl:* This bowl of questionable age, probably made between 1910 and 1920, definitely is not an early product. The glass has a very marked bluish cast and rings surprisingly well with a deep gong-like tone when tapped. The depth of the bowl is 3″ and it is 8¾″ wide across the top. 129b. *Stippled Roses Bowl:*

This is a late comer to the Milk Glass world, even later than the Dutch Windmill pattern. The usual 3″ depth and 7¾″ opening. The outside of the bowl is decorated with large open rose blossoms on a stippled surface. This is no antique prize.

130. *Swimming Swans Compote:* A close-up view of the Swimming Swans Compote showing the accurate detail of this popular and well-known pattern. Do not confuse this with the Swan and Cattail pattern being reproduced by the Westmoreland Glass Company. These patterns are distinctly different. This compote is 4¾″ tall with a 7¾″ bowl.

131. *Cut Star Bowl:* This rather attractive Cut Star bowl comes in milk white and in blue Milk Glass. There are three rows of finely cut stars around the upper part of the bowl and another row completely around the bottom. Sauce dishes can be found to match the bowl. 3¼″ high to the top of its scalloped edge. 7¼″ is the diameter of the bowl.

132a. *Beaded Rib Flared Top Bowl:* The flared top of this Beaded Rib bowl adds a pin wheel effect to its appearance. 10½″ from edge to edge and 3¾″ deep. The outer rim is beaded and the sides are ribbed. 132c. *Gothic Bowl:* A low bowl in the Gothic pattern which was used also for many sizes of plates. 8½″ in diameter and only 2¼″ deep. Manufactured by the Canton Glass Co. It is rare. Rather than a ring when tapped, it just gives off a dead clunk sound. 132b. *Shell Footed Oblong Bowl:* This bowl looks much longer than its 10″, and is 5¾″ across the middle. This pattern comes in a great variety of pieces and frequently had hand-painted decorations in the center panel.

133. *Knobby-Edge Bowl:* Millard refers to this bowl as *Knobby-Edge.* It seems as good a name as any for this rather difficult-to-describe border. This is one that never had a cover. It is 3¾″ deep, 10¼″ long and 7¾″ wide. It has the usual Atterbury china-like glaze and is definitely one of their products.

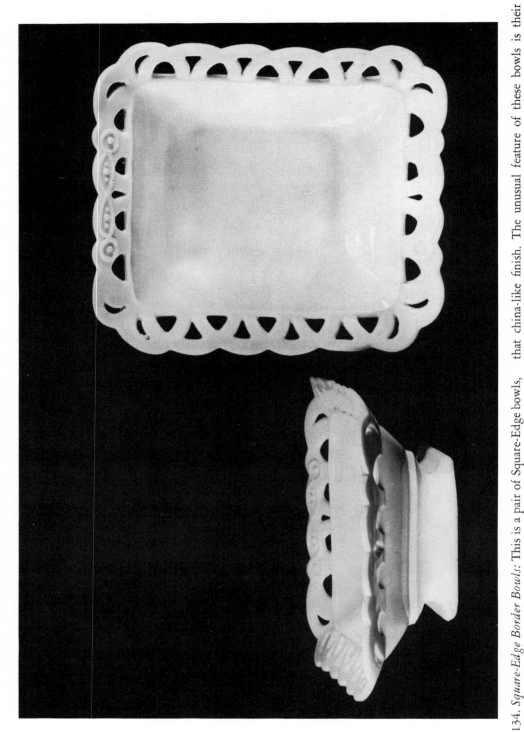

134. *Square-Edge Border Bowls:* This is a pair of Square-Edge bowls, 9¼" by 8¾". One is lying flat, the other is up-ended to give you a better view of the border detail. They are Atterbury products with that china-like finish. The unusual feature of these bowls is their shape which is almost square Most Milk Glass bowls are either round or oval.

135. *Lacy Crimped-Edge Dishes:* Look very carefully at these two Lacy Crimped-Edge dishes. Not a pair, both were made by Atterbury. The one on the left has its side edges turned up, the dish on the right has its side edges turned down. Both pieces were probably made in the same mold and this up and down side edge turning was accomplished by a "finisher" after the pieces had been removed from the mold and were still hot enough to be pliable. Sizes, both the same, 10" long by 6¾" wide.

136. *Square Lacy-Edge Bowl:* An Atterbury bowl, 3¼″ deep by 9½″ by 8½″. This photograph of the interior shows the snowflake beauty of its Lacy-Edge border. There is another bowl with this same Lacy-Edge border, same size, with the only difference being that the edges are crimped.

149

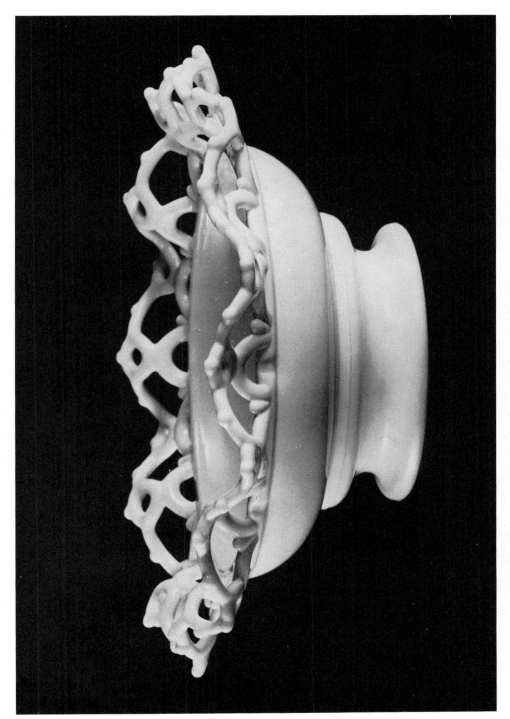

137. *Crinkled Lacy-Edge Bowl:* These Atterbury bowls were popular in the 1880's and are even more popular today, when they can be found. If you were to measure this bowl you would find it to be 8¾″ across the top and a full 3½″ deep.

138a. *Crimped Pin Wheel Border:* Do not confuse this border with the very similar Beaded Rib pattern. Somewhat alike in appearance, they are two distinctly different patterns. On this border there is no beading at all. It is 4″ tall and 8″ across. I have observed other bowls in this pattern with painted designs on both outside and inside. 138b. *Open-Edge Beaded Rib Bowl:* This bowl rings like a church bell when tapped. It is fairly deep, nearly 4½″, its width across the top is 9″. The top beaded rim has a permanent wave.

139a. *Lacy-Edge Base for Chicks:* This bowl or base is found as is, or with a top consisting of a pile of eggs and with a chick coming out of a large egg on top of the pile. I have learned from persons who purchased this bowl when it was originally made that it was available with or without the top. High quality Milk Glass, 3¾″ tall by 7″ across the top.   139b. *Chain and*

Petal-Edge Bowl: This low footed bowl is 5″ tall and 7″ across. It originally had an attractive hand-painted inside flower decoration. The Chain and Petal pattern is found on many Milk Glass pieces—plates, compotes, bowls, etc. This piece has a great many black particles imbedded in the glass.

Chapter Six

Covered Animals

BEAVERS, lambs, bears, camels, shrimp, quail, foxes, roosters, fish, horses, Pekingese, chows, turkeys, rabbits, bulls, hens, frogs, dogs, swans, boars, cats, cows, eagles, dolphins, turtles, deer, robins, doves, lions, elephants, and many, many other subjects quite as diversified have been subject matter for the covers of Milk Glass dishes.

Some are large, some are small; mostly they are milk white, but a few are black (deep amethyst) while others are blue and white. There are blue hens with white heads; a dog, half blue and half white; or a black hen with a milk white head. Some of the large covered Milk Glass hens have deep blue or amber heads, with milk white bodies; others have bodies in which the glass was marblelike blue, brown, green or orange. There are a few all-blue covered animals, notably the small hen, cat and dog dishes.

At the Redford Antiques Show outside Detroit I saw a McKee Covered Squirrel in gray on a split ribbed base. A short time later I found a gray Squirrel Top without the base. This, of course, is extremely rare. I have never seen this gray color in any other Milk Glass animals.

Some of the finest examples of the covered animal dishes were produced at the McKee Brothers factory in Pittsburgh, Pa. Often these animals were marked "McKee" on the base, and naturally such marked pieces are much sought after by collectors and bring higher prices than the unmarked pieces produced at the same factory.

The famous Atterbury ducks, which were patented, were outstanding specimens of the glassmaker's art of the 1880's and were, of course, a product of the Atterbury Company of Pittsburgh, Pa. They came in various colors and color combinations: white, blue, amethyst, white with amethyst head, white with blue head, etc. All of the Atterbury ducks seem to have been produced from the same (or identical) molds. I assume this because they followed the exact design of Patent No. 17192 obtained by T. B. Atterbury, March 15, 1887.

By far the most popular subject of the covered dishes is hens with a limited number of roosters supplementing them. This is accounted for by the fact that vast quantities of Milk Glass hens were distributed as premiums just before the turn of the century.

You will often find imprinted on the bottom of the base of certain pieces *Pat.* followed by the date, the month and the year the patent was granted.

Several of the covered animal dishes are known to be of foreign manufacture. The hump-backed Camel is reported as definitely English. The Frog and the large Turtle are reputedly French, and the Robin on the pedestal nest is a Vallerystahl (French) piece. However, the great majority of covered Milk Glass animal dishes are as American as the Fourth of July.

There is one debatable subject among collectors and dealers alike in regard to covered animal dishes. Just what top goes on which base or bottom? The trouble is that both dealers and collectors are uncertain. They find a covered animal tucked away on some pantry shelf; the present owner claims that it belonged to good old Aunt Het or that husband's grandmother told them she bought it full of mustard when she was a girl. The top apparently fits the base and the subject matter patterned on the base looks as though it corresponds with the cover. But often as not you get the piece home and another collector drops in, only to shout, "That isn't the base that goes with that cover." And then the battle is on.

As you will note, many of the covered animal dishes in this book belong to other collections and they appear just as their owners matched them up. Later investigation showed several tops were on the wrong bases. These have been noted in the captions. As far as I have been able, I have tried to get the covers on the correct bases. You must realize we had very little to use for actual comparison. There are few cuts and few photographs to judge from and the memory of man is short at best. Septua- and octogenarians who believe they can recall what fitted what are a bit vague when pinned down to facts. So if we have erred on occasion, please forgive us.

Strangely enough, you can find two or three times as many animal covers as bases. One day I heard a plausible explanation from a little old lady who owns an antique shop, and who from her many years of experience has acquired knowledge and lore far beyond my limited ability to absorb.

It seems that during the early 1900's canaries and other small birds were all the rage and that many a bottom of a Milk Glass covered dish was put in the bird cage to serve as a bath for the feathered darlings. The cover was tenderly laid to rest on the topmost shelf of the pantry, there to gather dust and age properly; while its counterpart led a much more active, though shorter, life in the bird cage. The longer I look for these hard-to-find bases, the more faith I have in the little old lady's theory.

*140. *Tall Covered Rooster:* This was originally a French product, not too early, but nevertheless an interesting specimen for collectors. The Westmoreland Glass Company now produces it so well that it is most difficult to distinguish the reproduction from the original. The reproduction comes either with or without a bright red comb. The early ones were all white.

141. *Chick and Eggs Covered Dish:* A unique Atterbury covered dish with the usual Atterbury Lacy-Edge base. The top is distinctive, consisting of a pile of eggs with a chick emerging from the top egg. Made during the 1880's, popular then, rare now. *From the collection of Mrs. Maud Doyle, Mt. Vernon, Ohio.*

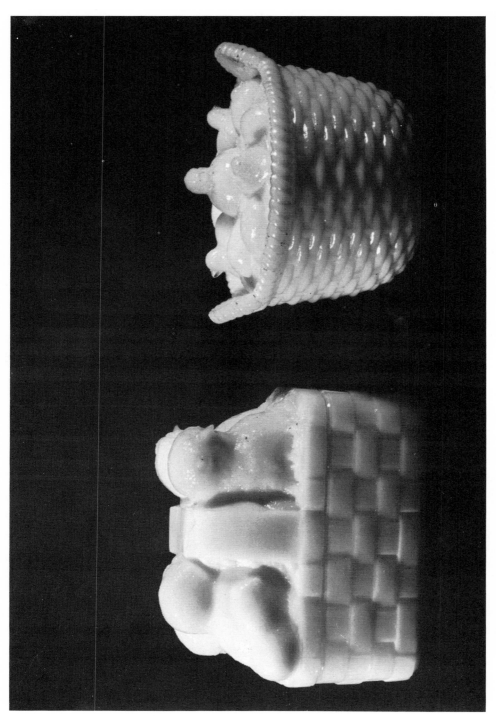

142a. *Square Basket with Chicks:* This small covered square basket of chicks is only 2¾″ wide by 4¼″ long and 3½″ high. The detail is very good including the pointed beaks and the little combs atop their heads. The little basket is well done and the weave design is excellent. 142b. *Chicks on Round Basket:* A small 3″ high basket, 4½″ from handle to handle. The basket top shows a setting of eggs in the process of hatching, little chicks popping out everywhere. The top had the usual covering of gilt specks. This was an attractive child's piece.

143a. *Vallerystahl Hen on Basket:* The Milk Glass has the marked grayish coloring typical of most French Milk Glass. 7½″ in length, a full 5½″ across the base and 6″ tall at the tail. *Vallerystahl* appeared on the upper surface of the basket floor.   143b. *Vallerystahl Breakfast Set: Vallerystahl* appears inside the hen on the basket base, on the top surface of the 11″ by 10″ tray, on the inside bottom of each egg cup and on the inside bottom of the little covered basket salt. Lavish use of paint was made.

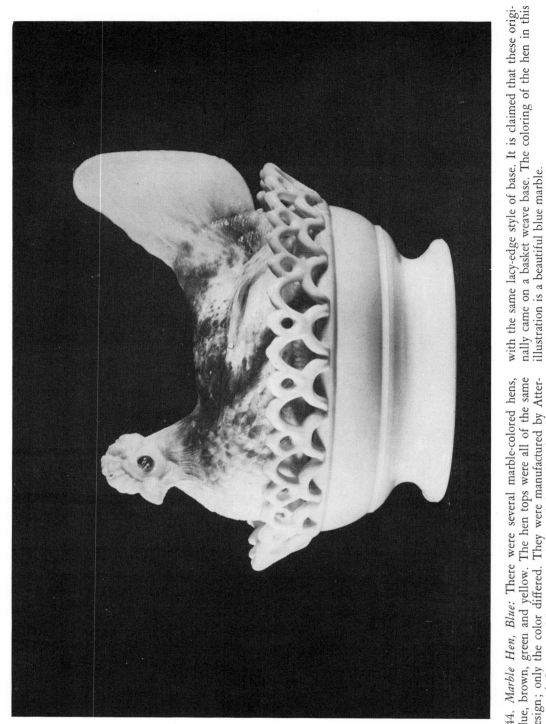

144. *Marble Hen, Blue:* There were several marble-colored hens, blue, brown, green and yellow. The hen tops were all of the same design; only the color differed. They were manufactured by Atterbury and Company. The great majority of those found today come with the same lacy-edge style of base. It is claimed that these originally came on a basket weave base. The coloring of the hen in this illustration is a beautiful blue marble.

145. *Straight Head Hen:* The name derives from the fact that this hen looks straight ahead rather than at the usual angle. Note the different style basket base. This hen apparently had glass eyes at one time, but they were missing when I found it.

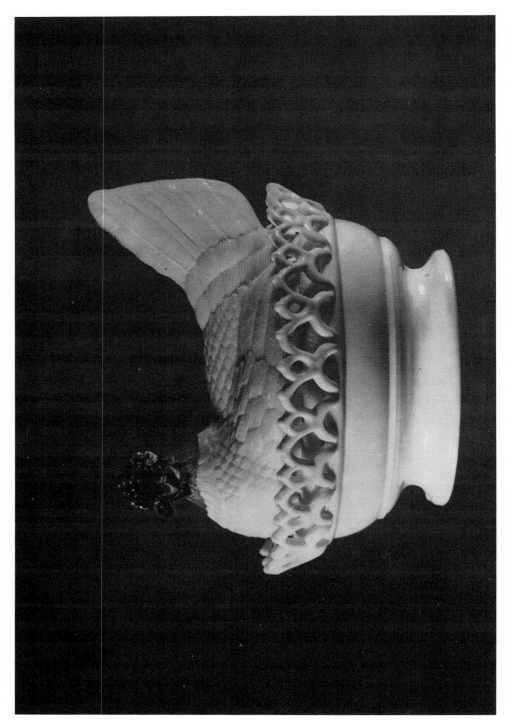

146. *Amethyst Head Hen Lacy Base:* Another typical Atterbury hen. This one has an amethyst head. I have also seen them with blue and amber heads. They all have the usual Atterbury Lacy-Edge base. *From the collection of Mrs. Maud Doyle, Mt. Vernon, Ohio.*

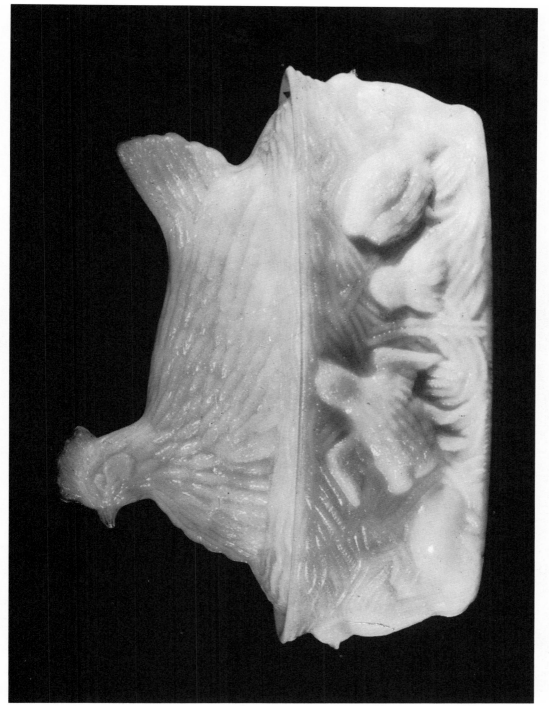

147. *Hen on Chick Base:* This is a Flaccus piece showing a hen on the nest with a highly decorated base depicting baby chicks in action. The hen details and workmanship does not compare with the Atter- bury pieces—but it is a pleasant change to see a base without the lacy-edge. Length, 6¼″.

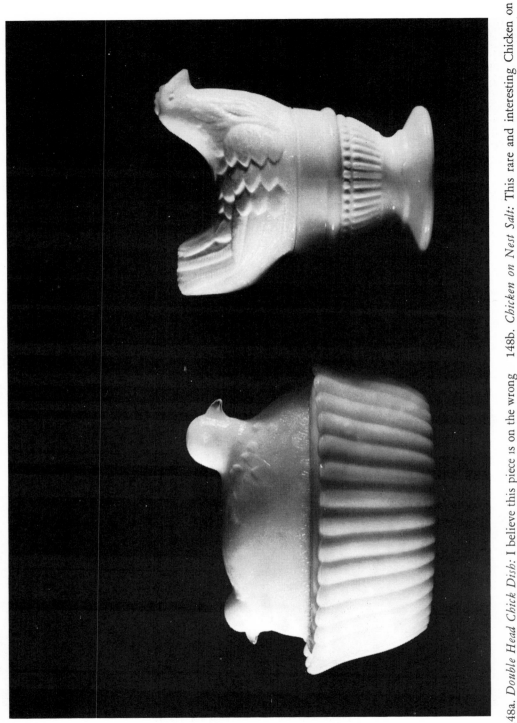

148a. *Double Head Chick Dish:* I believe this piece is on the wrong base. Millard shows it on a basket weave base, and I believe he is correct. This Double Head Chick top fits its ribbed base perfectly but something looks wrong. As it appears here, it is part of a famous collection whose owner claims it to be correct, but I am going to string along with Mr. Millard and recommend the basket base.

148b. *Chicken on Nest Salt:* This rare and interesting Chicken on Nest Salt came in blue and in white Milk Glass. It is very much a collector's piece, difficult to find. It is approximately 3½″ tall and 2¾″ wide across the back of the hen, head to tail. *Both from the collection of Mrs. Maud Doyle, Mt. Vernon, Ohio.*

149a, b, c. *Two Black Hens and a Cow:* The black Milk Glass hen is placed on her proper basket weave base. The rare black Milk Glass cow is on an unusual base. The black hen with the milk white head is very rare. It came in several combinations. *149a, b, c. *Two Hens and a Rooster:* The hen on the basket weave base and the rooster are being manufactured today by Westmoreland. The little hen in the middle on the split rib base is old. It is milk white with a blue head. This, it has been contended, should be on a basket base. Since she fits snugly and looks well on her present nest and, furthermore, since she's been there for years, let's let her stay there. *All from the collection of Mrs. Maud Doyle, Mt. Vernon, Ohio.*

150. *Wavy Base Duck:* This is a large duck, a member of the Farmyard Assortment by Challinor, Taylor and Company, on a distinctly different type base. The base has a broad ¾″ rim around its top with a wavy pattern on both surfaces of the rim to represent ripples of water. The duck is 8½″ long, the base 6″ across and the entire piece, cover and all, 5¼″ high. You often see this duck brilliantly painted in the bright colors of wild duck feathers. One of the most attractive of the duck patterns. Its realistic glass eyes give an added touch.

*151a. *Milk White Atterbury Duck:* This Atterbury duck is entirely milk white. It is identical with the all blue duck on Illustration 151 B. The glass eyes are golden brown with a blackish center. The sharp detail of these Atterbury ducks is one of their outstanding features. The molds that produced these specimens were made by experts. The difference between the reproduction and the original is that the former lacks a patent date or *Pat. Pend.* on bottom of base.

151b. *Atterbury Blue Duck:* Here is one of the famous blue ducks patented March 15, 1887, by Thomas B. Atterbury. It is a beautiful light blue with red glass eyes. Size, 11″ from tip of tail to point of beak. This duck was made in various color combinations, in all milk white, all blue or all amethyst. It is very rare and brings top prices. *Both from the collection of Mrs. Maud Doyle, Mt. Vernon, Ohio.*

152a. *Basket Base Duck:* An odd little duck about which little is known. Milk white. 152b. *McKee Horse on Split Rib Base: A & B* from the collection of Mrs. Maud Doyle, Mt. Vernon, Ohio. 152c. *Amethyst Head Atterbury Duck:* The rarest of the ducks.

*153a. *Raised Wings Swan No. 1:* Compared with B, A is more compact, has a shorter neck, shorter wings and the base on which the swan is resting rises higher in the chain-edge bowl. You will note this swan has large glass eyes. This is worth remembering, for there is a reproduction manufactured by Westmoreland that looks very similar but has small painted eyes. 153b. *Raised Wings Swan No. 2:* This swan has been hand painted slightly and some of the soft shaded colors look like shadows in the illustration. This swan, too, has glass eyes. *Both from the collection of Mrs. William Bullock, Toledo, Ohio.*

154. *Swan On Water:* This is one of the rarest of the swan covered dishes. The cover represents a swan on the water, on which two fish may be seen. The base is unusually deep and heavily decorated with cattails, Christmas trees, flowers and bulrushes. This lovely piece is found in both blue and white Milk Glass. *From the collection of Mrs. Maud Doyle, Mt. Vernon, Ohio.*

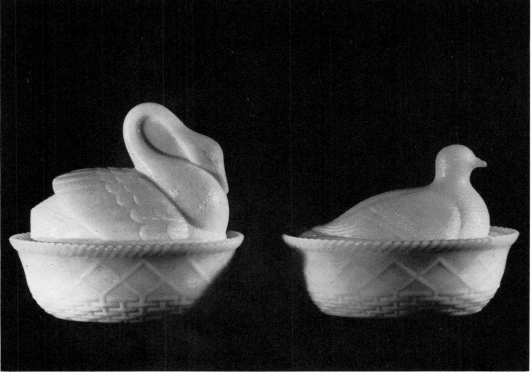

155a. *Knobbed Basket Weave Swan: Patent Applied For* appears on the inside of the cover. 6¼″ tall with a base length of 7″. On the unusual base raised knobs intermingle with the basket weave design. 155b. *Closed Neck Swan:* Should be on a split ribbed base. 155c. *Dove Cover Dish:* Should also set on a split ribbed base. *B and C from the collection of Mrs. Maud Doyle, Mt. Vernon, Ohio.*

156. *Mother Eagle Cover Dish:* One of the truly fine pieces of Milk Glass. The artist who designed this graceful cover created one of the top ranking Milk Glass pieces of all time. If a group of experts were to select the ten best in Milk Glass I believe this selection would be on every list. It is a rare and high-priced covered dish. Made by Challinor, Taylor and Company, it was featured in their catalog under *Farm yard Assortment. From the collection of Mrs. Maud Doyle, Mt. Vernon, Ohio.*

157a. *Robin on Nest Dish:* This photograph, taken at a slightly different angle from the same piece in B, causes the bases to appear different. Their manufacture is credited to the Indiana Goblet and Tumbler Co. This one has all its war paint. A rare piece at a high price. *From the collection of Mrs. William Bullock, Toledo, Ohio.* 157b. *Robin on Nest Unpainted:* Without the paint it may be seen that the flower design work on the base is well executed and that the Milk Glass is top quality. Would you believe that both were produced from the same mold?

158. *Melon with Leaf and Net Covered Compote:* This compote comes small, medium, and large. The little Melon finial atop the cover is an outstanding characteristic of all covered Melon pieces. Note the very marked difference in the surface design of this leaf and net pattern as compared with the plain Melon pattern which, unlike the net design comes in covered sugar, creamer, covered butter and spooner. *From the collection of Mrs. Dale Myers, Howe, Indiana.*

159. *Setter Dog Covered Dish:* This is a man's piece of Milk Glass, the hunting dog, the gun and the game pouch, produced by Flaccus. It measures 6¼″ lengthwise. Note the rounded outlines typical of Flaccus pieces, which do not have the sharp clear-cut detail of McKee or Atterbury products. *From the collection of Mrs. William Bullock, Toledo, Ohio.*

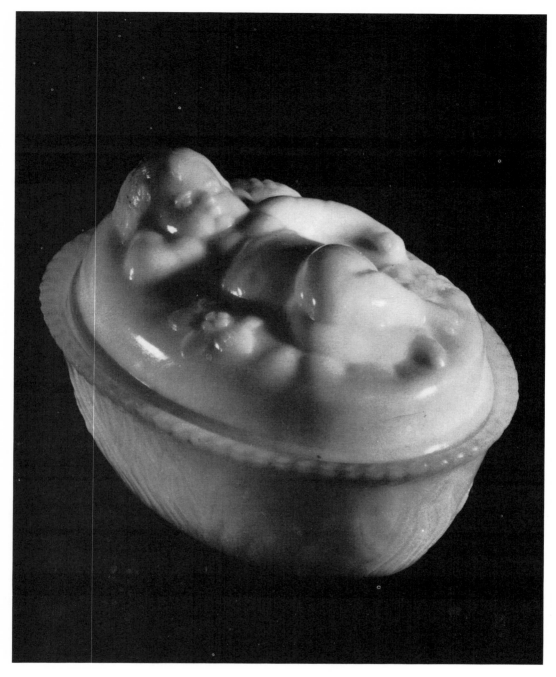

160. *Moses in the Bulrushes:* There is considerable opalescence to this little 5½″ covered dish, and the piece does have charm. Because of the angle of this photograph the bulrush detail on the base is not as clear as I should like to show it.

161a. *Dewey on Round Basket Base:* An unusual pink cast to the Milk Glass. In this bust Dewey's hair is parted in the center. Base is 4½″ at the top, height of entire dish, 5½″.

161b. *Dewey Tile Base:* Dewey's hair is parted on the right side of his head. The base of this dish consists of a brick wall. 6½″ long, 4″ tall by 3¼″ across the center.

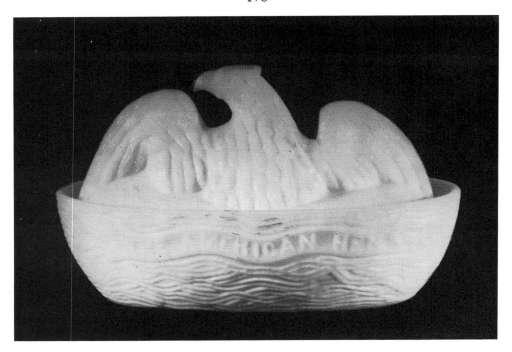

162a. *The American Hen:* The American Hen is the wording on the banner strip along the top of the base. The cover shows an American Eagle, wings spread to protect three large eggs inscribed: *Porto Rico, Cuba, Philippines.* The date of manufacture was 1898. Underneath the base are the words, *Patent Applied For. 6″* long by 4″ high. 162b. *Battleship Maine:* This is a craftsman's idea of what the Battleship Maine looked like, lacy curtains at the windows and all. It's 7½″ long by 3½″ tall to the top of her main stacks. *Maine* may be seen at the front of the upper deck. On the base is the figure 5, evidently for factory records.

163a. *Entwined Fish Covered Dish:* Fish at their best—even when made by Atterbury—are not too enticing a subject in glass. Base is usual Atterbury Lacy-Edge bowl. A rare piece. *163b. *Hand and Dove:* In the ring on the finger was a piece of colored glass representing a precious stone. Although the bird frequently had a glass eye, it is missing in this piece. The original of this is rare and high in price. The reproductions are fairly plentiful; look out for them. An Atterbury creation, 8¾″ in length, 4¾″ tall. *Both from the collection of Mrs. Maud Doyle, Mt. Vernon, Ohio.*

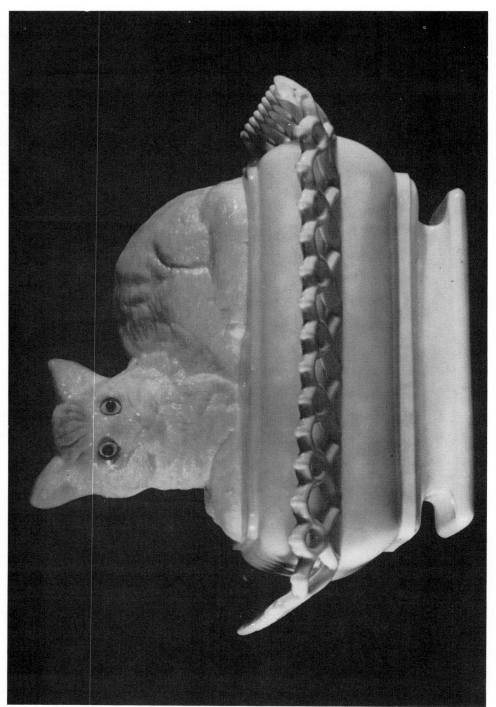

164. *Lacy-Edge Cat:* Those glass eyes really look natural on this Lacy-Edge Cat covered dish. One of the Atterbury and Company animals with its corresponding rectangular Lacy-Edge bowl base. Date, the 1880's. Length of bowl base 8″. *From the collection of Mrs. Dale Myers, Howe, Indiana.*

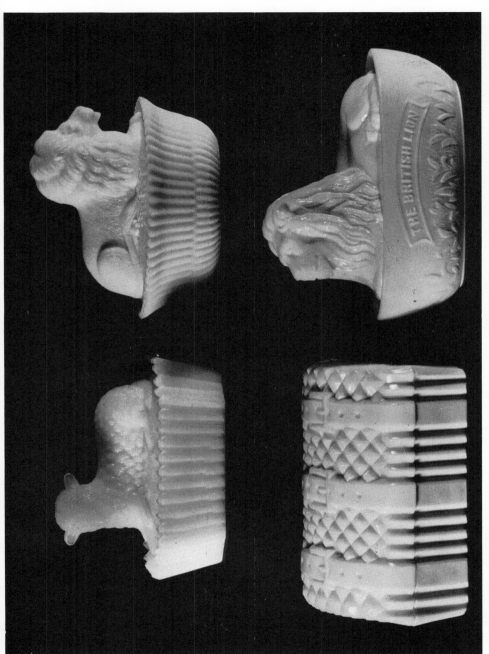

165a. *Woolly Lamb on Octagon Base:* The coarse ribbing on the octagon base looks not unlike a picket fence. The mold maker created good detail on the body of the lamb, but the head is rather indistinct and fuzzy. 5¼" in length. 165b. *McKee Lion Split Rib Base:* Like nearly all of the McKee covered pieces this Lion covered dish shows good detail and proportions. The split-ribbed base is practically a McKee trade mark. 5½" long, good quality glass. 165c. *Trunk*

With Straps: A late piece attributed to the French. Heavy, with the slippery glaze of modern pieces. Watch out for this piece and don't pay more than a gift shop price. 165d. *The British Lion:* There can be no argument as to the name of this Milk Glass covered dish, for it is emblazoned in a banner strip across the front. *A, C, and D from the collection of Mrs. Maud Doyle, Mt. Vernon, Ohio.*

166. *Majestic Lion Covered Dish:* The handsomest of all the Lion covered dishes. A rare piece for the finest collections of Milk Glass. This is also the tallest Lion covered dish. Note the beautiful design workmanship on the base. *From the collection of Mrs. Norma F. Moebus, Lima, Ohio.*

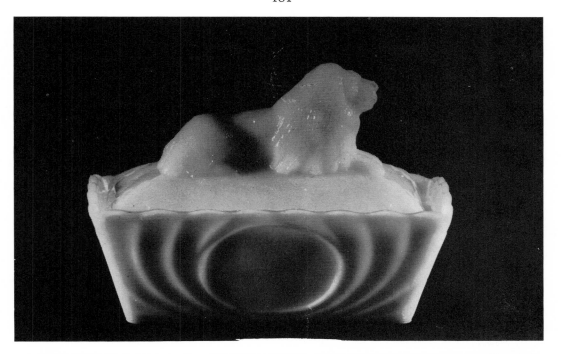

167a. *Lion Scroll Base:* 5¾" long. Nothing exceptional in design or subject. 167b. *Fish Covered Dish:* Manufactured by Challinor, Taylor and Co. in the 1880's. The large glass eyes give the fish a rather knowing look. The fish rests or supports itself on its fins. 167c. *Ribbed Lion Covered Dish:* This Ribbed Lion is often found on different bases. The base shown in this picture definitely matches the ribbing on the cover. However, very frequently this top is found with a typical Atterbury Lacy-Edge base. Since these Lion-covered dishes were manufactured by Atterbury, it is only logical to assume that they could have been sold originally with either base. *All from the collection of Mrs. Maud Doyle, Mt. Vernon, Ohio.*

168. *Ribbed Lion on Lacy Base:* This is the back view of the Ribbed Lion reposing on the Atterbury Lacy-Edge base. Both the Ribbed Lion top and the Lacy-Edge bases are products of the same manufacturer, and frankly I have seen more Ribbed Lion covers on Atterbury Lacy-Edge bases than I have on the matching ribbed bases. So let the collectors argue out the right or wrong of the case. I merely present the facts for your information. *From the collection of Mrs. Maud Doyle, Mt. Vernon, Ohio.*

169. *Ribbed Fox Covered Dish:* Here is a Ribbed Fox top on a matching ribbed base. An Atterbury product, it also comes on the Atterbury Lacy-Edge base. You will note this fox lacks a glass eye. These covered animal dishes were furnished with or without glass eyes at a slight price differential. Also the glass eyes were very easily lost. *From the collection of Mrs. William Bullock, Toledo, Ohio.*

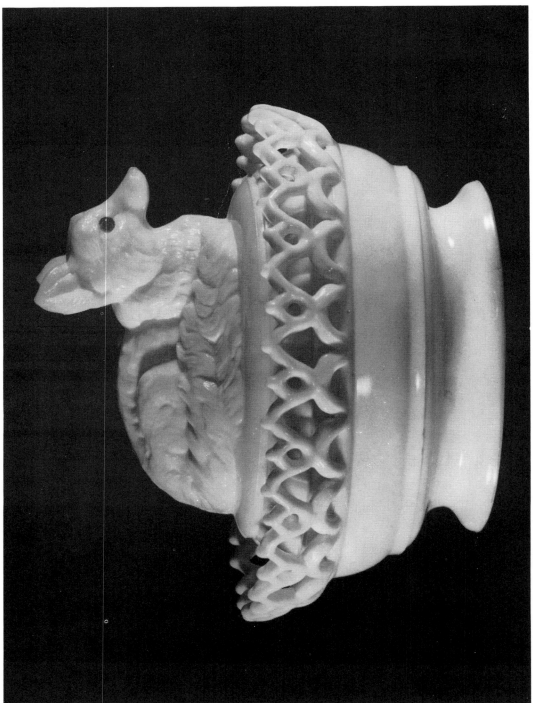

170. *Ribbed Fox on Lacy-Edge Base:* Some collectors will insist that this Ribbed Fox cover is on the wrong base. Millard shows this combination of Ribbed Fox top on an Atterbury lacy-edge and I am inclined to think he is correct. I have seen the Ribbed Fox top on both types of base many times and all three parts—the Ribbed Fox top and the separate bases—were manufactured by Atterbury. *From the collection of Mrs. Maud Doyle, Mt. Vernon, Ohio.*

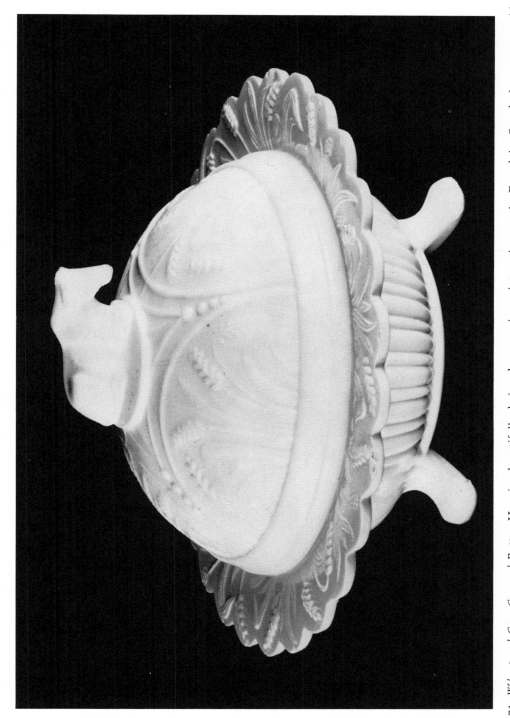

171. *Wheat and Cow Covered Butter:* Here is a beautifully designed cover is an interesting touch. Found in Canada last summer, this covered butter in chalk white Milk Glass. The mold design on the piece has all the earmarks of English manufacture. base is much clearer than that on the cover. The cow finial atop the

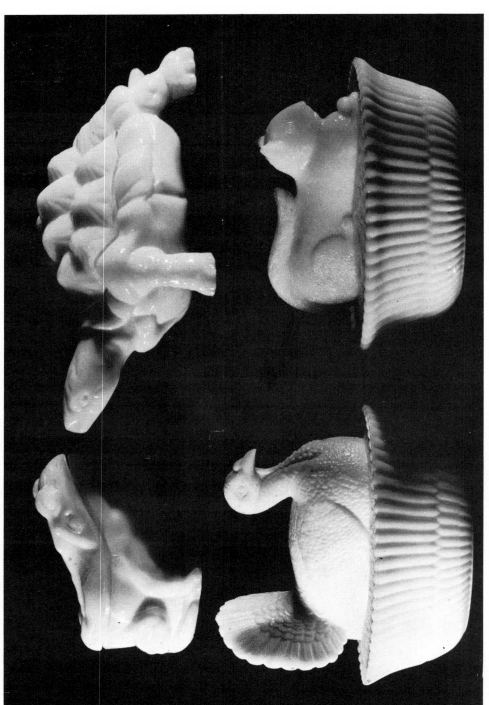

172a. *Sitting Frog:* A modern piece found in many collections and in many antique shops. It has a shiny glaze finish and is slippery as an eel. Any collector should be able to recognize that this was made recently, probably by Vallerystahl in France. 172b. *Knobby Backed Turtle:* Another contribution to the Milk Glass field, slippery, shiny glaze, completely new looking. No one, not even a novice, should be fooled by it. It's very heavy. Of French origin, probably Vallerystahl.

*172c. *Turkey Cover Ribbed Base:* One of the rarest of the McKee covered dishes, brings top prices wherever found. Has the McKee base measuring 5½" in length. 172d. *Squirrel Cover on Split-Ribbed Base:* The accepted split-ribbed base identified with McKee, whose pieces were not as large as the Atterbury animals. 5½" long. *All from the collection of Mrs. Maud Doyle, Mt. Vernon, Ohio.*

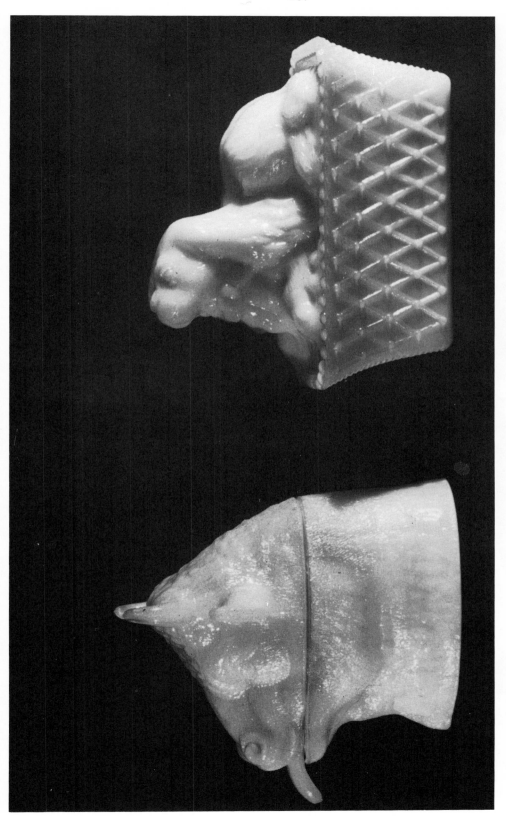

173a. *Bull's Head Mustard Jar:* This Bull's Head Mustard Jar is a popular piece with collectors. It was made in blue and in milk white. Often, the little ladle, which served a double duty, both as a tongue in the bull's mouth and, for more practical use, as a ladle to dish the mustard from the jar, is lost. 173b. *Pekingese Dog Cover:* This snooty Pekingese with the upturned nose is resting on a very flossy base befitting his dignity. It is a small covered dish measuring 3½″ by 4¾″. Considerable opalescence to the glass and very excellent molded detail on the base design. Ruth Webb Lee in her book *Victorian Glass* states: "The dog is one of the exceptionally few animal dishes we can positively attribute to Sandwich." *Both from the collection of Mrs. Maud Doyle, Mt. Vernon, Ohio.*

174a. *Deer on Fallen Tree Base:* The edge of both top and base of this piece, produced by Flaccus, are fiery opalescent. Detail is typical of Flaccus mold makers and artists. Rare. Length, 6¾″. *From the collection of Mrs. William Bullock, Toledo, Ohio.* 174b. *Dog Cover, Half-White, Half-Blue:* There were several different color combinations of these Dog covers. The bases are plain except for the wide ribbing. 174c. *Cat Cover, Blue Body, White Head:* Must have been designed by the same craftsman who created the Dog covers. 5½″ long. *From the collection of Mrs. Maud Doyle, Mt. Vernon, Ohio.*

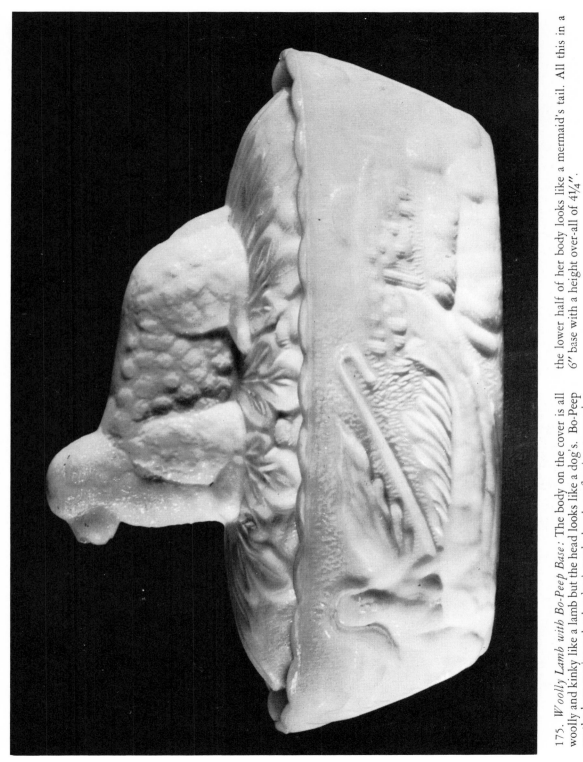

175. *Woolly Lamb with Bo-Peep Base*: The body on the cover is all woolly and kinky like a lamb but the head looks like a dog's. Bo-Peep on the base carries a shepherdess' crook, has long flowing tresses but the lower half of her body looks like a mermaid's tail. All this in a 6″ base with a height over-all of 4¼″.

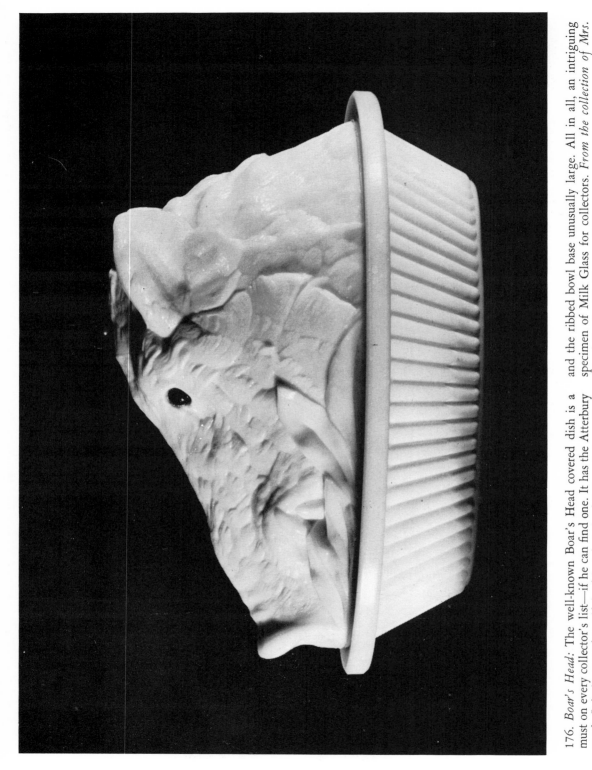

176. *Boar's Head:* The well-known Boar's Head covered dish is a must on every collector's list—if he can find one. It has the Atterbury touch. It isn't a very beautiful subject, but the detail work is excellent and the ribbed bowl base unusually large. All in all, an intriguing specimen of Milk Glass for collectors. *From the collection of Mrs. Maud Doyle, Mt. Vernon, Ohio.*

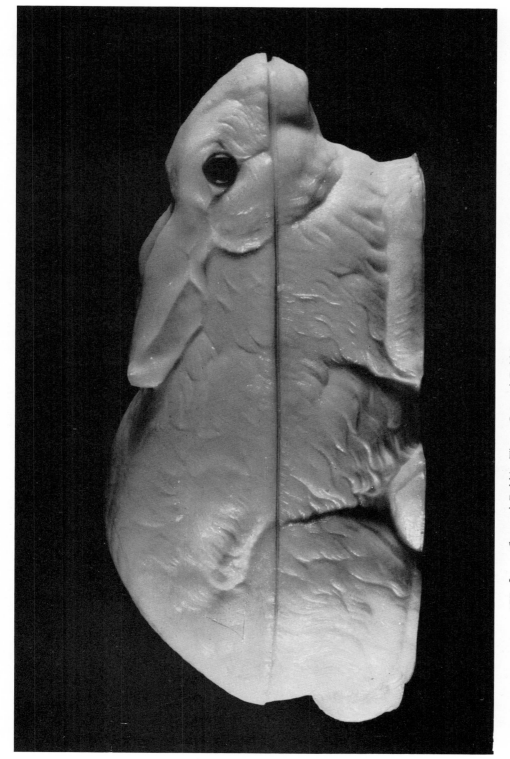

177. *Large Covered Rabbit:* These Covered Rabbits came in three sizes: large, medium, and small. They are good-looking pieces of Milk Glass, well designed, correct proportions, accurate in detail. The large glass eyes give them a very life-like appearance. Of all the rabbit pieces in Milk Glass these large covered rabbits are the most popular.

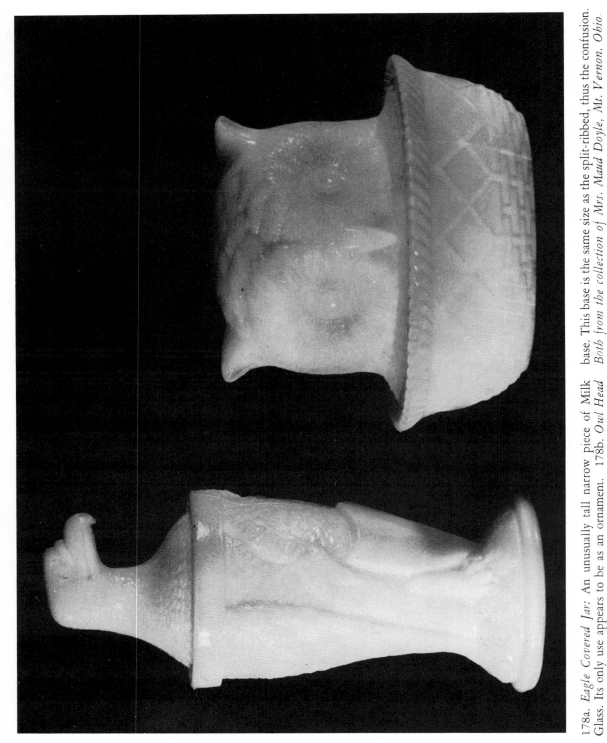

178a. *Eagle Covered Jar:* An unusually tall narrow piece of Milk Glass. Its only use appears to be as an ornament. 178b. *Owl Head Covered Dish:* An Atterbury Owl which belongs on a split-ribbed base. This base is the same size as the split-ribbed, thus the confusion. *Both from the collection of Mrs. Maud Doyle, Mt. Vernon, Ohio.*

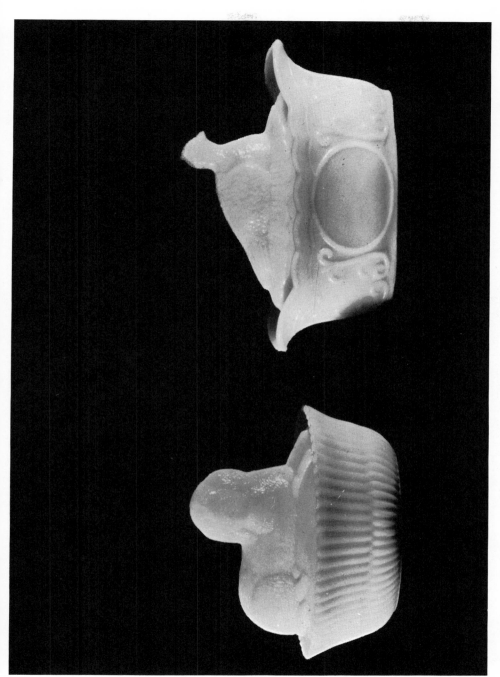

179a. *White Dog Covered Dish:* A white nondescript dog on a McKee base. These same dogs, hair for hair, have been reposing on a fairly wide-ribbed base. It is too bad that the principle used for hens by one manufacturer was not universally applied. Matching covers and bases were numbered similarly, e.g., cover 1 belonged to base 1. *From the collection of Mrs.*

Maud Doyle, Mt. Vernon, Ohio. 179b. *Quail Cover Dish:* The Quail cover dish has a base all its own, decorated with an oval on each side and scalloped work around the ends. The mold detail is very limited on both the cover and the base. The quality of the workmanship does not compare with the Atterbury or McKee pieces. 6½″ long by 4½″ tall.

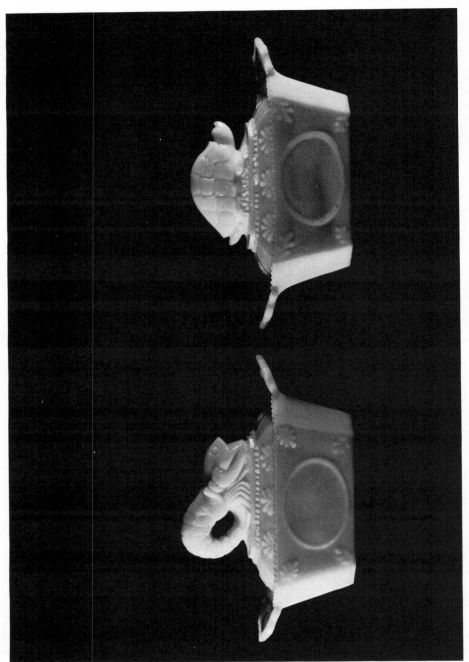

180a. *Crawfish Cover:* A companion piece to the Turtle cover dish. Identical base, same quality of glass, definitely created by the same artist at the same factory—just which factory we have been unable to discover up to the present writing. The little end handles are clever.
180b. *Turtle Cover Dish:* Here is a covered animal dish made by neither Atterbury nor McKee. The turtle top is well designed, with good mold detail and nice proportions. The dish underneath is rather plain—an oval centered on the sides, parallel narrow ribbing on the ends with little handles or lips at each end for holding or picking up the piece. 4¼″ tall by a full 7¼″ handle tip to handle tip. *Both from the collection of Mrs. Maud Doyle, Mt. Vernon, Ohio.*

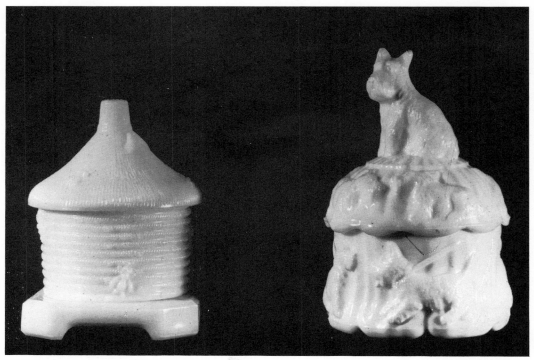

*181a. *Mule-Eared Rabbit Dish:* The ribbed base is octagonal. Height, 4½″ length, 5½″. 181b. *Bee Hive Cover Dish:* A modern piece. Antique shop price, $8.00; gift shop price, $1.50. 181c. *Scotty Dog Cover:* So new it is marked *Made In U.S. of America. From collection of Mrs. Maud Doyle, Mt. Vernon, Ohio.*

182. *Tall Owl Jar:* This handsome fellow with the white chest and tremendous claws is exactly 7″ tall and 3¼″ across. Made by Atterbury. *From the collection of Mr. Ralph Miller, Dalton, Ohio.*

*183a. *Resting Camel:* Originally English. 6¼″ long, 5⅜″ high.   183b. *Pintail Duck:* 5¼″ long, 4¼″ high. Millard quotes as Westmoreland but shows McKee base.   183c. *Vallerystahl Swan:* 5¾″ long, 5½″ tall.

184a. *Dewey on a Battleship Base:* 5½" long, 5" tall. Good quality Milk Glass, but not rare. 184b. *Cruiser Type Warship:* The many Milk Glass ships made after the Spanish-American War look so much alike but do differ. Even though this ship looks similar to that shown on Plate 300 of Millard's book *Opaque Glass*, a second glance will show considerable difference. 6" long, 4" high.

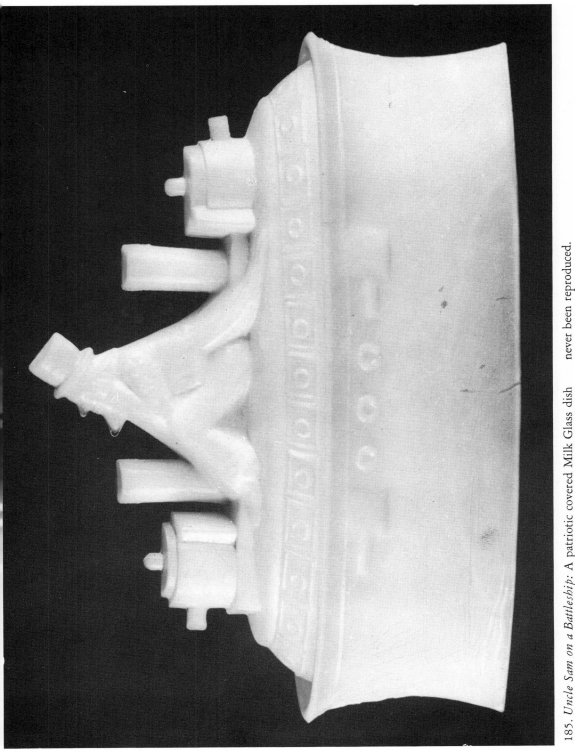

185. *Uncle Sam on a Battleship*: A patriotic covered Milk Glass dish of 1898 and 1899. 4½″ high, 6½″ long. As far as I know this has never been reproduced.

186. *Atterbury Square Block Swan:* Like all Atterbury products this Swan is outstanding. The mold marks are very distinct. In fact, they are so deep that the piece resembles cut glass. The rim of the base consists of alternating plain and ribbed square blocks. The piece is very heavy because of the thickness of the glass. It measures 8″ long by 6½″ tall at the bend of the Swan's neck. This Swan which may be found in clear pressed glass as well as milk white is rare in either. *From the collection of Mrs. Maud Doyle, Mt. Vernon, Ohio.*

Chapter Seven

Miscellaneous

SELECTION and elimination were the hurdles to overcome in this chapter. There are literally hundreds of small Milk Glass pieces in every shape, form or style. There are small covered boxes or jars, hanging match holders, innumerable small pin trays or ash trays, and gadgets by the score. One could devote an entire chapter to salts and peppers. However, since the scope of any one book is limited, here I have tried to show and describe those Milk Glass pieces most important to the collector. Perhaps another book incorporating the little things that are to be found in the nooks and corners of the antique world may be in order at some time in the future.

In this chapter are to be found some fine examples of Milk Glass. The pair of early lamp chimneys with the original Ben Franklin labels still attached are rare and unique. There is a large black Milk Glass swan, extremely graceful in design. I have observed this same-size swan in white, but its design and mold markings indicated that it was of a considerably earlier period.

Unusual are two hand dishes, Victorian to their fingertips, and excellent examples of the period. Two hands cupped together make a little calling card tray or dish. On the forefinger of the hand holding the fan is a bright red piece of glass representing a ruby. Then there is the very desirable pair of open sleigh salts, not to be confused with the fairly common small sleigh bases for the Chicken or Santa Claus covers. The open sleighs are distinctly salts and never had covers.

Two gadgets are a small box in the form of a royal coach, and a card container for a pack of playing cards.

In addition to the above this chapter includes many more of the odd pieces that do not fall into the larger categories.

187. *Jewel Celery:* Comes in yellow (not Custard Glass), blue and purple slag. I have never seen it in milk white, although I believe that it does come in white. Frequently a piece of colored glass was placed in the design on the sides, thus giving the piece its name.

188. *Pair of Early Lamp Chimneys:* The diamond-shaped labels with the imprint of Ben Franklin on them are almost as interesting as the Chimneys themselves. *Lead glass guaranteed* is printed on the upper part of the label and *G. & S.* at the bottom. These chimneys are chalk white Milk Glass with a ruffle-top edge. A rare pair which makes a perfect match for the early oil Milk Glass lamps.

189a. *Pair of Sleigh Open Salts:* A pair of extremely rare Milk Glass open salts. Approximately 4″ long, 2½″ across the top. They never did have covers. 189b. *Santa Claus on Sleigh:* A small 5½″ covered sleigh dish with a Santa Claus cover. *189c. *Hen on Sleigh:* This little Hen on a Sleigh is a Westmoreland piece. *B and C from the collection of Mrs. Maud Doyle, Mt. Vernon, Ohio.*

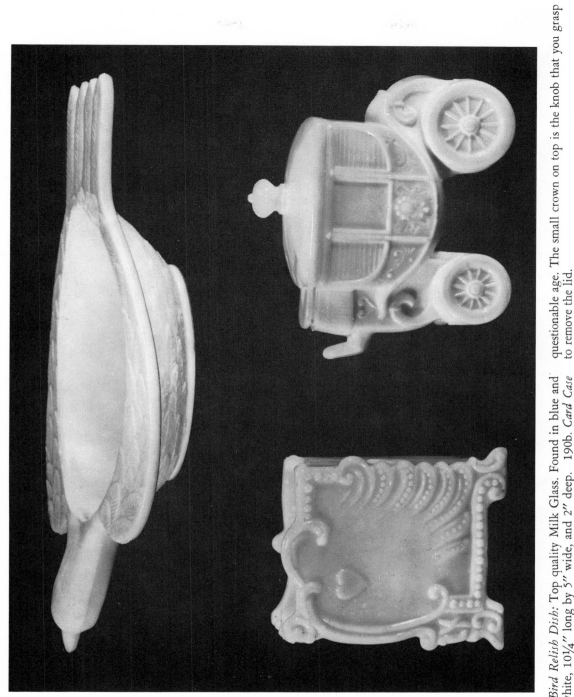

190a. *Bird Relish Dish:* Top quality Milk Glass. Found in blue and milk white, 10¼" long by 5" wide, and 2" deep. 190b. *Card Case Holder:* Note the heart marker on the side. 190c. *Royal Coach:* Of questionable age. The small crown on top is the knob that you grasp to remove the lid.

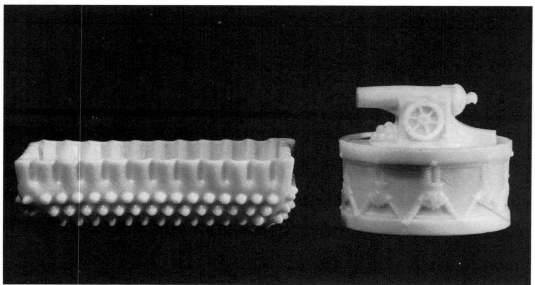

191a. *Saturday Night Bath:* Rare and unusual. *From the collection of Mrs. William Bullock, Toledo, Ohio.* 191b. *Hob Nail Ruffled Dish:* 6¾″ long, 4½″ wide, 2″ deep. 191c. *Snare Drum Cannon:* 4″ tall, 4½″ wide.

192. *Milk Glass Castor Set:* A silver castor set with Milk Glass containers, one each for salt, pepper, mustard and salad dressing. Almost puritanical in its severity. The only ornate design is on the silver feet. The Milk Glass is plain as a plaster wall.

193. *Hand and Fan Dish*: The outstanding detail and design, and the fine quality of the glass in this Hand and Fan dish indicate the manufacturer—Atterbury. Set in the ring on the finger is a piece of brilliant red glass. The feathered edge, the ivory slats, the fringed tassels are all excellently detailed. Size, 9″ in length. *From the collection of Mild ed Flach, Piqua, Ohio.*

*194. *Double Hands with Grapes:* This Double Hands with Grapes card tray was originally created by Atterbury. Because of the excellence of the current reproduction, it is difficult to distinguish it from the original. Size is 7½" in length by 5¾" from thumb to thumb.

195a. *Versailles Dresser Jar:* A close-up view of the typical dresser hair box in the Versailles pattern.   195b. *Three Little Glass Hats:* These small Glass Hats were made from a tumbler mold. They were molded into the form of an ordinary drinking glass and, still hot, the glass was worked into various hat shapes.

196a, b. *Two Dresser Jars:* These were used by women when hair was worn waist-long. The combed out hair was saved in them. The pattern on the left is a Scroll Variant, the one on the right is called Ray. Two well-known Milk Glass patterns for dresser trays, button boxes, hair boxes, etc. 196c, d. *Actress Covered Jars:* Used on the dresser for various purposes. The heads of women, said to be prominent actresses of the gay nineties, decorated the covers. The glass is poor quality with a marked grayish cast to it. *C and D from the collection of Mrs. Norma F. Moebus, Lima, Ohio.*

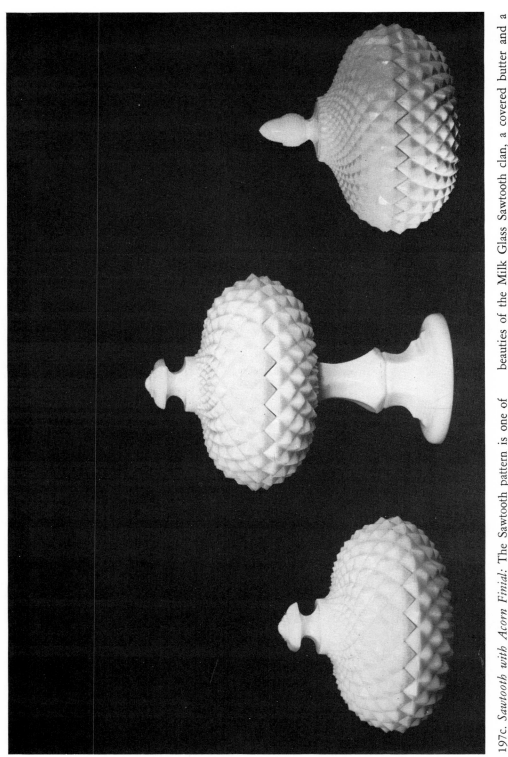

197c. *Sawtooth with Acorn Finial:* The Sawtooth pattern is one of the very earliest produced in Milk Glass, one of the rarest and one of the most difficult to find. Look carefully at the acorn finials atop the covered pieces. Not all Milk Glass covered pieces show the acorn. There is also the hexagon finial which is shown in the next illustration. 197a, b. *Sawtooth with Hexagon Finial:* Here are two more beauties of the Milk Glass Sawtooth clan, a covered butter and a small-footed compote. The finials on the top of the butter and compote are hexagon in shape and are found on many of the covers of early pressed glass patterns. The acorn finial was also a popular cover decoration on the early pressed glass covers, as well as on Milk Glass pieces.

198. *Roman Cross Butter, Sugar and Creamer*: One of the few patterns in Milk Glass available complete with sugar, butter, creamer and spooner. Above are shown three pieces of the set. The design of this pattern seems to fade and then reappear as you look at it. It is necessary to concentrate in order to distinguish the small Roman Crosses from which the pattern derives its name. A rare pattern not too easily found these days.

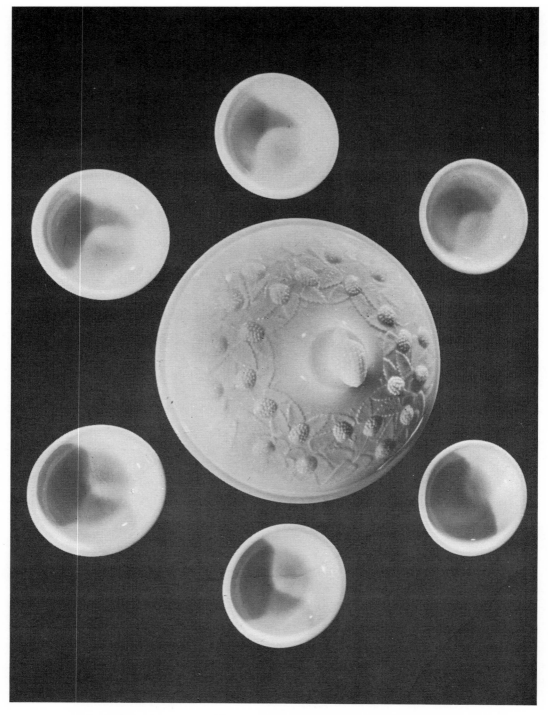

199. *Blackberry Compote and Six Sauces:* This is a bird's-eye view of Blackberry which is a well-known and popular Milk Glass pattern available in most pieces for a table setting.

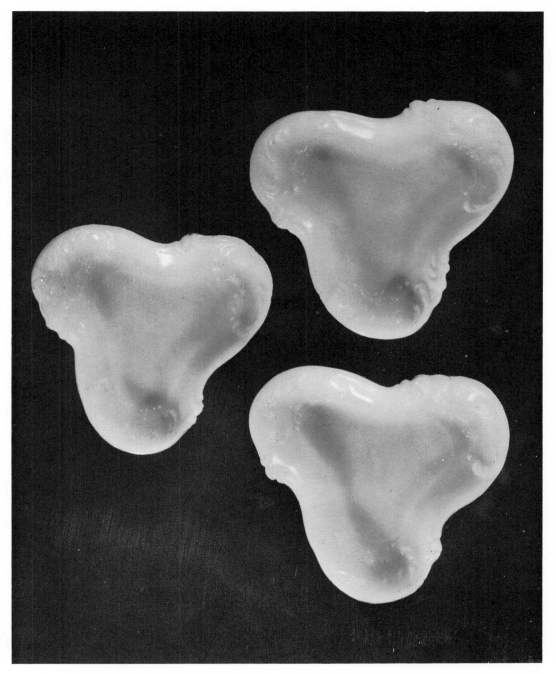

200. *Scroll Variant Triangular Sauces:* Scroll Variant is not especially
rare, for it comes often on pin trays or dresser ornaments and the
quality of the glass is rather mediocre, but the triangular shape of
these sauces was unusual and different.

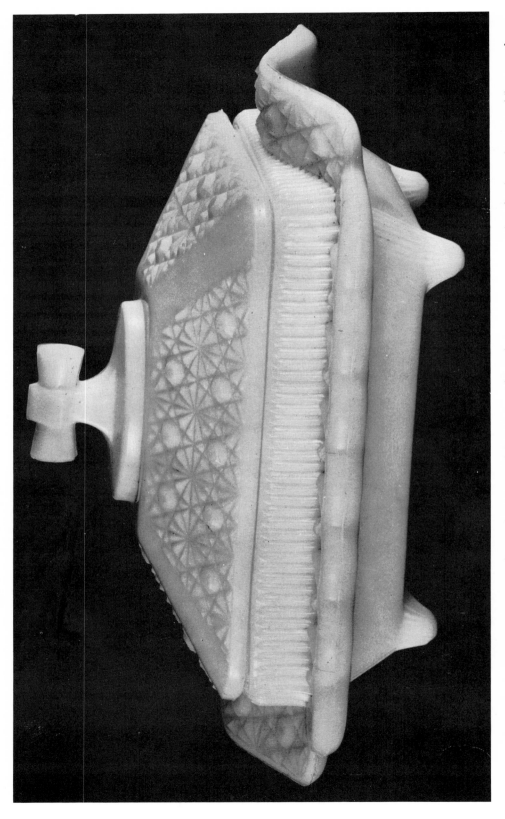

201. *Daisy and Button Butter Rectangular*: A fancy covered butter, in the old familiar pattern, Daisy and Button. This pattern is found frequently on various Milk Glass pieces and oftentimes on the underside of butter dishes, relish dishes, etc. This butter is 7½″ long, 5½″ wide, and 4½″ to top of cross bar finial on the cover. The curved ends used as handles are unusual, as are the knobs of each corner which act as feet and raise the base well off the table.

202a. *Daisy and Button Square Butter:* The shapes used for this pattern seem endless. 7¾″ by 5″ to top of knob. 202b. *Jacob's Coat But-ter:* A rare piece of Milk Glass in this clear pressed glass pattern. 5½″ across, 5″ tall.

203a. *Diamond and Fan Butter:* A butter in a very little-known pattern. 7″ across, 6¼″ high. 203b. *Scroll and Leaf Butter:* 5½″ in diameter, 4″ tall. Pattern greatly resembles well-known Princess Feather design and is frequently mistaken for it.

204a. *Indian Head Match Holder:* This is a large match holder, built for the big telephone pole matches that pipe smokers use. It was not a wall piece but stood upright on a brace back of its own. 5″ tall, 4¾″ wide. Good quality Milk Glass and fine design detail.   204b.

Fish, Pickle Waffle Type: This fish, made by Challinor, Taylor and Company, has small white glass eyes with black centers. Size, full 9″ long and 3″ high, by 4¼″ across. Very fine mold detail, made from top quality white Milk Glass.

205a. *Vallerystahl Tray with Egg Cups:* This is the tray that had the big red covered hen on it. The reason it is shown again is to give better view of the tray, the little rooster egg cups and the covered basket salt. *205b. *Basket Weave Basket, Plain:* Westmoreland who originally produced this basket still manufactures it. The top and base of the basket is very often painted. 5″ across, 4″ tall. 205c. *Emerging Chick on Basket:* A flat circular area appeared on front of this basket which was sold primarily as a premium. Space for the advertising label had to be provided.

206. *Cosmos Silver Pickle Dish:* The combination of silver and Milk Glass is rare. A pattern used with more diversified pieces than any other.

207a. *Waffle Design Sugar Shaker:* 207b. *Milk Glass Spittoon* (*Mickey*).

208a, b, c. *Three Miscellaneous Pieces:* Oval Medallion, Acorn, Apple Blossoms: A is a spooner. B is a small Sugar base. Note the net background. C is a jar or spooner. The band around the top is pastel yellow, pink, blue or gray. 208d, e. *Beaded Scroll* and *Wide-Ribbed Small Butters:* D is 4¾″ across, 3¼″ tall. E is 5¼″ across, 3½″ tall. Quality of glass in D and E is excellent.

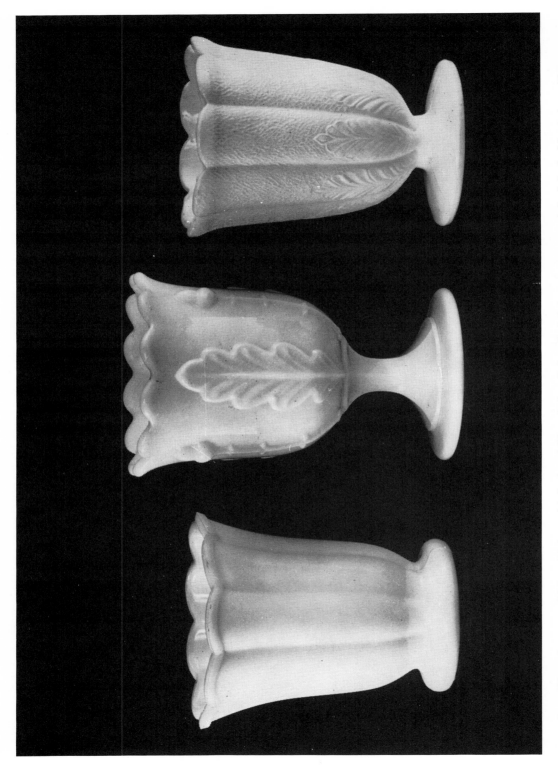

209a, b, c, *Three Spooners: Melon, Melon with Leaf and Net, Oak:* A is the Plain Melon pattern. All covered pieces in this pattern have the little melon finial on the cover. Patented November 8, 1870. B is called Oak, portrays an oak leaf flanked by twigs with an acorn at the end of each twig. C is the rare Melon with Leaf and Net pattern, patented April 23, 1878.

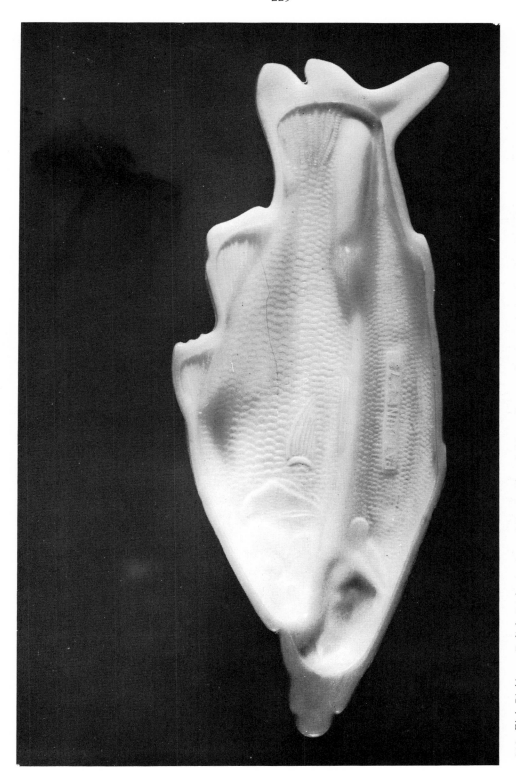

210. *Fish Pickle or Relish Dish:* A view of the inside of this well-known Milk Glass Pickle or Relish Dish. It is inscribed, *Pat. June 4, '72.* The underside (not shown) is more ornately decorated than the top and also has four little knobs or feet that raise the dish from the table. The dish is 11″ long by 4½″ wide.

Chapter Eight

Sugar Bowls

SOME of the most exquisite examples of the Milk Glass craftsman's art are found among sugar bowls. For sheer line of beauty, charm of design and firm chalk white glass consistency, the sugar bowls are in a class apart.

In this chapter creamers and covered butters are shown with sugar bowls only because they have identical patterns.

There are several well-known pressed glass patterns among the sugar bowls, as, for example, the Princess Feather design.

One of the noteworthy features of sugar bowl covers is the knob, or finial. The variation in the size and shape of this appendage, its harmony with over-all design of the cover and its general decorative effect make it worthy of careful observation.

One of the loveliest sugar bowls to be found anywhere is the exceedingly rare Cameo. The delicate workmanship of the leaf decoration, the small beads of the circles and the cameo heads on the bowl and cover are pure art.

A majestic bowl is the Beaded Circle covered sugar. Charm and grace are its outstanding characteristics. The bead designs in the circles have the appearance of strings of pearls.

Another of the debatable questions among Milk Glass collectors is whether or not there are open sugars. Probably 75 per cent of the antique dealers would claim that there are. My own opinion is that coverless sugars were never made. Whenever I have come across one and was given sufficient time to search for the cover, I have been able to find it. In this chapter I have shown a few open sugars—only because they are recent purchases whose tops I have not yet had time to find. In the past I have picked up a base in Indiana and the matching cover in eastern Connecticut. I do believe that ultimately I will come upon the covers for all of my "open" sugars.

211. *Diamond, Fan and Leaf Sugar:* In Chapter VII there is a butter with the same design on the cover. The finials on the two are identical, and the consistency of the glass is the same. Unusually tall—7½", and 4¾" wide at opening.

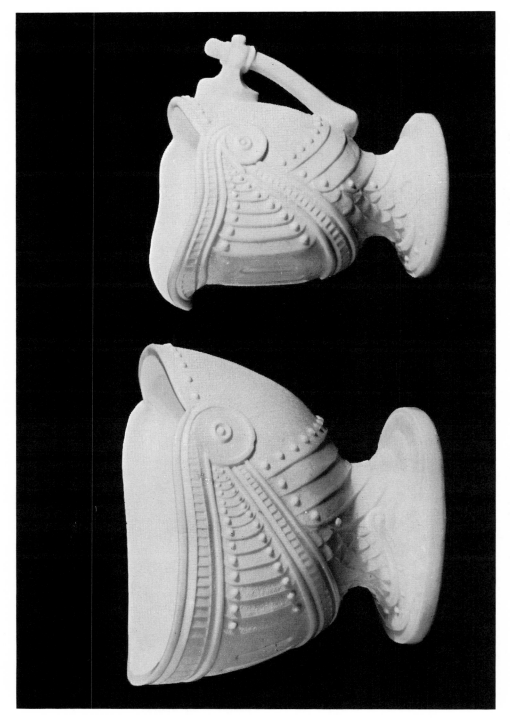

212. *Casque (helmet) Sugar and Creamer:* These two pieces are so English they practically say "Cheerio!" The workmanship of both sugar and creamer is correct down to the very finest detail. Note how small the creamer is in relation to the sugar.

213. *Plain Melon Sugar and Butter:* The Melon pattern shown in this picture is absolutely smooth, as compared with the Melon with Net and Leaf on the compote in Chapter V, which looks exactly like a muskmelon fresh off the vine. Both, however, have the same finial—a little melon.

214. *Diamond Point and Leaf:* The glass of this sugar has an unusual gray cast. It is a tall, good-looking, well-designed covered sugar bowl. This pattern is rare and seldom found.

215. *Princess Feather Sugar Bowl:* Here is royalty in appearance as well as in name. This beautiful and rare piece of Milk Glass is one of the most desirable of clear pressed glass patterns but a piece of Princess Feather Milk Glass is a find indeed.

216. *Early Loop Sugar, Sandwich:* Sandwich Milk Glass is a rarity itself. There are mighty few covered sugars with acorn finials. The glass contains bluish black shadow effects found in no other Milk Glass but Sandwich. Held up to the light there is a fiery opalescence, another Sandwich Milk Glass trait. This bowl is 7¼″ tall to tip of finial and 4″ across at the widest point.

217. *Cameo Sugar Bowl:* This Cameo covered sugar is one of the most beautiful specimens of Milk Glass that I have ever seen. The design is outstanding. 7¼″ tall to the top of the lady's head and 4¾″ wide at the cover edge.

218. *Beaded Circle Covered Sugar:* 7¼″ tall, cover and all, and slightly over 4″ at the widest point. A row of beaded circles goes completely around both the cover and the bowl proper. Considerable fiery opalescence in the glass.

219. *Honeycomb Sugar:* Approximately 11″ in height and 4½″ in diameter. Extremely heavy. Recent. Oiliness and smoothness indicate 1920 or later origin.

220. *Daisy Whorl Sugar:* The Daisy Whorls of six each to the cover and the bowl furnish the name for this Milk Glass sugar bowl. It is tall, 9¾" high, and 4½" across.

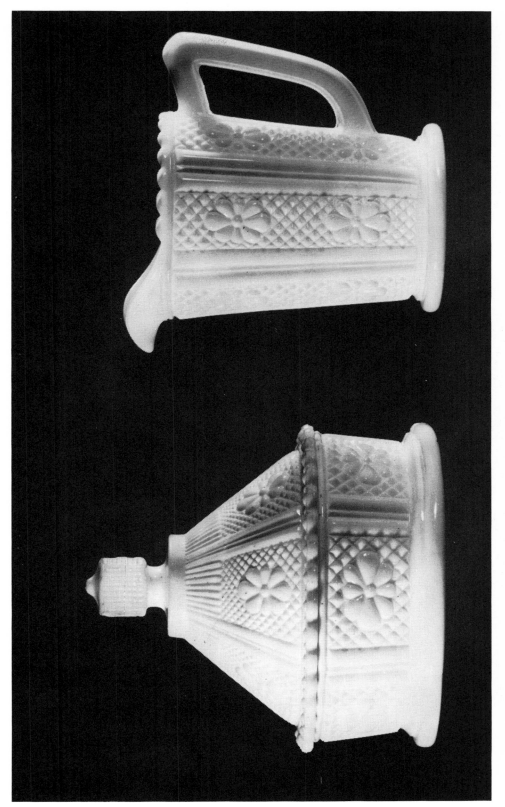

221. *Paneled Flower*: I admit that the covered piece resembles a butter dish considerably more than a sugar bowl. It was inadvertently photographed with the creamer in this chapter, but in order to show this lovely pattern it was not eliminated. The pattern is found most frequently in milk white or purple slag.

*222c. *Beaded Jewel Sugar:* A John Kemple reproduction made from original pressed glass mold. 222d. *Holly Sugar Bowl:* Here is a really beautiful Milk Glass sugar bowl of English ancestry. It has the typical English chalk white Milk Glass, with fine design detail. There are two different Holly patterns in Early American pressed glass, but this piece does not match either. Not quite 5¼″ tall without cover, and about 4½″ across the top. 222a, b, *Basket Weave Sugar and Butter:* Practically all pieces may be found in this pattern. Patent date, June 30, 1874. 6″ tall, 4½″ wide. Neither rare nor high quality glass.

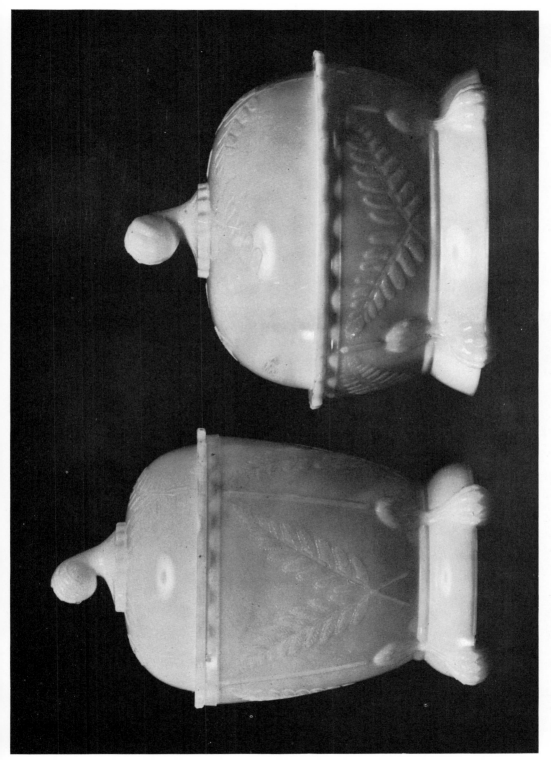

223. *Crossed Ferns—Ball and Claw Sugar and Butter:* Do not confuse this Crossed Fern pattern with the Crossed Fern design in
Chapter V. Note the Ball and Claw motif, an important feature of
this pattern which does not appear in the other. Texture of glass and
general make-up lead to the conclusion that this is a contemporary
of the famous Melon patterns.

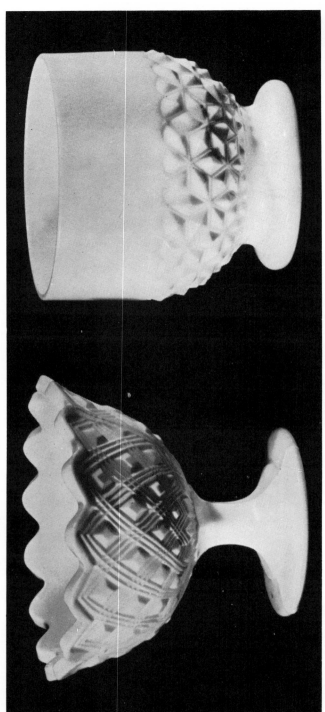

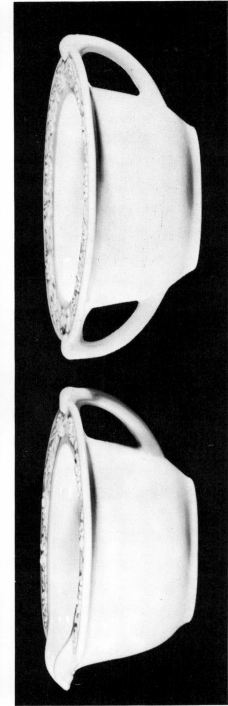

224a. *Plaid Sugar Base:* Quality of glass very good, mold design, clear and distinct. Slightly over 4″ tall. 224b. *Star Diamond Sugar Base:* An outstanding sugar bowl. Base 4⅛″ tall minus cover. Glass is creamy milk white. 224c. *Flower Rim Sugar and Creamer:* Based on shape, type of glass content and floral design rim I believe that this pair is relatively recent.

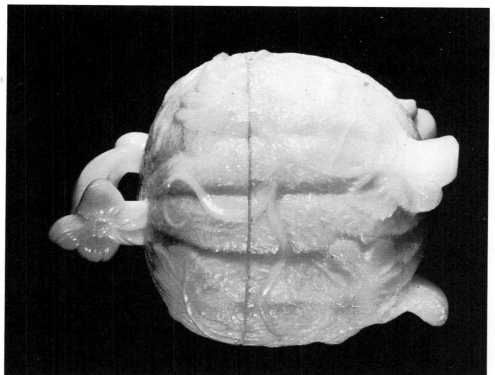

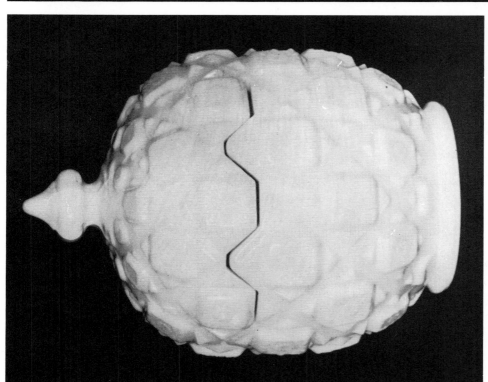

*225a. *Westmoreland No. 500. Covered Sugars* (*Block and Fan Variant*): The glaze is so apparent that this piece is frequently mistaken for Ironstone china. It is easily recognized as a new piece.

225b. *Trumpet Vine Sugar:* An English covered sugar that looks far more French than English, has the slurred design effect and has a grayish texture. Very heavy and thick. Height, 6″, diameter, 4½″.

226. *Hexagon Block Sugar:* Extremely heavy glass with a very deeply cut design makes this handsome piece. 9″ tall, 5¼″ wide. From its dimensions it could be a large sugar or a small cracker jar.

227. *Ihmsen Sugar Bowl:* Millard shows this sugar bowl minus its top, and says: "A trail piece that is well known to dealers and collectors. It is rather scarce. It shows various figures on the panels." He calls the pattern *Ibsen.* I have yet to meet a dealer or collector who owned this piece or who had ever seen one other than in Millard's book, with the exception of the owner of the bowl in this photograph. She states it was manufactured by the Ihmsen Glass Company of Pittsburgh, Pa. and was a salesman's sample. *From the collection of Hood's Antique Shop, Mentor, Ohio.*

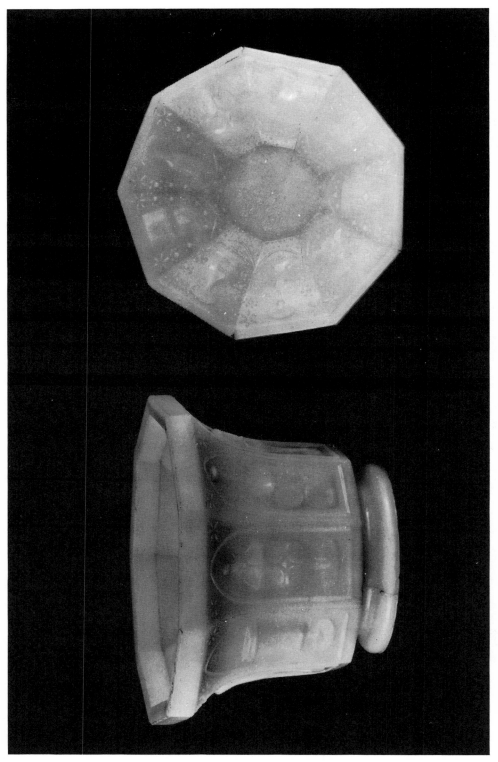

228. *Ihmsen Sugar Bowl and Cover:* Here is another view of the Ihmsen sugar bowl showing the bowl and the inside of the cover. Mrs. Hood tells me there were only about twelve or thirteen of these bowls made. They were salesman's samples that showed various items manufactured by the company. There were nine panels in each cover and base, portraying eighteen different items in the Ihmsen line. Another name for this sugar is Trade Bowl, because it was used to show the trade samples. This piece is a true rarity in Milk Glass. *From the collection of Hood's Antique Shop, Mentor, Ohio.*

229. *Pressed Threaded Sugar Bowl:* There is very little known about Pressed Threaded Glass. It was known to have been produced in clear pressed glass, but I believe this is the first example ever to be shown in Milk Glass. The pattern is simple—absolutely plain with the exception of parallel threads along the surface. Do not confuse this with the Nicholas Lutz Threaded Glass of Sandwich fame. His glass made during the 1870's was blown, this sugar is molded pressed glass. Nearly 7″ tall, it measures approximately 4½″ across. A rare sugar to find.

230. *Maple Leaf Sugar:* There are plenty of maple leaves on this bowl—six around the bowl, eight smaller leaves around the cover, and three around the finial topping the cover. A medium-sized bowl, 6½" tall by 4¼" wide. The pattern is lightly applied on bluish opalescent glass.

231. *Two Marble Sugar Bowls:* Unusual and interesting in Milk Glass are the marble sugar bowls whose texture is just like that of the marble Milk Glass hens. The open one on the left is blue marble, that on the right is barn red marble. Since the marble hens are attributed to Atterbury, it is safe to assume that these came from the same source.

232. *Double Loop Covered Sugar:* A striking example of an early Milk Glass sugar bowl with the popular acorn finial on the cover. This statuesque piece is Milk Glass at its zenith—the graceful lines, the deep cut design, the true proportions in height, width and depth. A rare early sugar, 8″ high, 4″ wide at the base and 4¼″ wide at mouth of bowl. The color is off-white with a slightly bluish cast.

Chapter Nine

Bottles and Vases

THE COLLECTOR of Milk Glass who special-izes in bottles will find the field strictly limited. Primarily the rare items are to be found among the commemorative bottles, the animal and bird bottles, the colognes and the flasks. There are many other items that interest collectors and that are shown and described here, but these categories make up the royalty of this field.

The rarest items are the commemorative bottles such as the Grant's Tomb bottle, the Statue of Liberty Base bottle, the tall Bunker Hill bottle and the extremely rare Columbus Column bottle with its original and unique metal top. A disturbing feature about these rare bottles was the apparent lack of harmony in the design of the lovely body and the ungraceful, protruding neck. However, the probable explanation for this lies in the metal topper which may be seen on the Columbus Column. This covers the ungainly neck thus bringing harmony to the entire piece.

The rare animal and bird bottles bring top prices, too. All come in white Milk Glass only, with the exception of the mineral water bottles which I have seen in white, black (deep amethyst) and deep bottle green.

Several examples of semi-modern whiskey and liquor bottles are included in this bottle chapter: first, because they are Milk Glass; secondly, they are found in antique shops being offered as antiques, and thirdly, bottle collectors collect them. I do not consider these bottles collector's pieces because of their youth and because they are still being produced. In antique shops they usually cost $5.00. My guess is that in a liquor store the same bottle may be obtained filled at this price.

Dresser bottles are rather common, having been manufactured by the thousands not too long ago. Most of them were flamboyantly decorated with various shades of paint which ultimately faded or flaked off. However, the condition of the paint provides a good in-dication of age for the collector.

In vases, white Milk Glass predominates, although blue occasionally turns up. In all my travels in search of glass I recall seeing no more than fifty pairs of blue vases.

At its best the field of Milk Glass vases is a limited one. Next to Milk Glass bottles there is the smallest selection to choose from. On occasion a choice piece of a desirable pattern does make its appearance. Also an alert collector can often recognize a good basic shape beneath some of the garish paint used on many. It is possible to remove the paint—a process requiring hours of soaking, scrubbing and scraping. The emergence of a graceful pair of vases makes all the labor well worth while.

233. *Yellow Pinch Bottle:* Yellow is one of the rarest shades found in Milk Glass. This bottle is almost a light lemon yellow but is not to be confused with the anemic yellow of custard glass. The round mushroomy stopper fits perfectly and matches in contour the general outline of this rare bottle. A full 9½″ tall by 4¾″ wide in the middle. Excellent quality Milk Glass. Rarely found.

234. *Columbus Column Bottle with Stopper:* Truly a rare bottle. I believe that most of the rare commemorative bottles had metal cover pieces. 13″ tall, the base, 3¾″ wide. With neck cover approximately 18½″ tall; figure of Columbus, 7″.

235. *Grant's Tomb Bottle:* Another of the rare commemorative bottles. This bottle has the long unsightly neck that at one time evidently en- joyed a metal cover of some sort. I have never found one with its original neck piece. Height, 8¼".

236. *Statue of Liberty Base Bottle:* Rare. On the protruding neck are two grooves for its metal top. Again, I have never found a cover. 10″ tall; base, 3¾″ wide. Metal cover probably 4″ to 5″ long. Memorial bottles came in milk white of top quality glass. Date, app. 1884.

237a, c. *Beaded Rib Cologne Bottles:* Choice collector's items. Early manufacture, neck opening very crude, glass content denotes regal ancestry. I have seen this same bottle in amethyst (pint size) and a large quart size in a beautiful early bottle green. 8″ tall, 2″ wide at the base.

237b. *Bunker Hill Bottle:* A replica of the monument of Bunker Hill. Very slender, 12″ tall, 2½″ wide at the base and tapers up to about 1⅛″ across at the base of the neck. A heavy bottle for its size, of very high quality Milk Glass. Extremely rare, much sought after by both Milk Glass and bottle collectors.

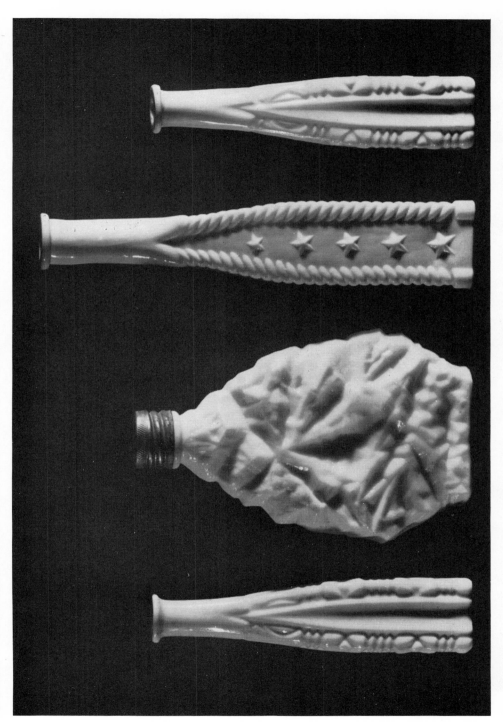

238c, a, d. *Five Star and Cable; Pair of Little Perfume Bottles:* Crude, early, rare would best describe these small milk white bottles. Held to the light, they show flashes of brilliant opalescence. So crudely made they can scarcely stand up straight. Each neck has a bend or twist to it indicating hand workmanship. The Five Star and Cable is 7½″ tall by 1½″ at the base, the little fellows are nearly 4¾″ high by 1¼″ across the bottom. 238b. *Klondike Flask:* An interesting little bottle, especially to bottle collectors. I doubt very much if it was produced during the gold rush days (1849) as claimed by Mr. Millard. The little Milk Glass produced as early as that was quite different in type and quality from the glass in the Klondike bottle. It is supposed to represent a gold nugget.

239a. *Dice Bottle:* Unique to say the least. On its base is inscribed, *Pat. March 24, 1891.* Frequently such patent numbers were set in backwards. *From the collection of Mrs. William Bullock, Toledo, Ohio.* 239b. *Novelty Milk Bottles:* The two smaller bottles are solid topped, the center neck has the opening and is the bottle proper. 4″ tall, 2¼″ wide at base. *T* is molded on the bottom. 239 c, d. *Japanese Bottles:* Strong Japanese influence—entire decorative scheme is Japanese. The glass is poor quality, grayish cast, milk white. Design is sloppy, lacking sharp detail. Evidently had stoppers. 7½″ tall, 4″ across base.

240a, b. *Duck Bottle, Plain Whiskey Bottle:* The Duck in contrast to the plain Whiskey bottle is very rare and was made of top quality white Milk Glass by Atterbury. It is 12″ tall and 3¾″ wide at the label. *From the collection of Mrs. Norma F. Moebus, Lima, Ohio.*

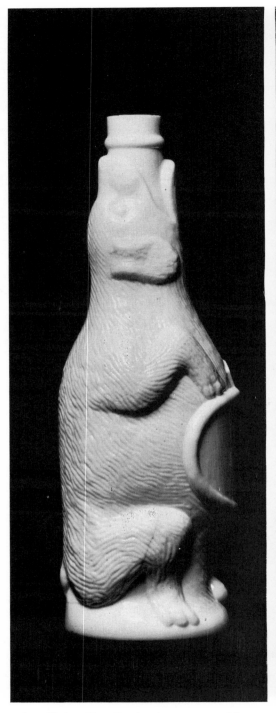

241a. *Sitting Dog Bottle:* A patent on this rare dog-shaped bottle was applied for by J. L. Dawes, but whether it was granted I do not know. It is heavy Milk Glass, 12″ tall and nearly 3¾″ wide at the label. A nice big bushy tail wraps half way around the dog's haunches.

241b. *Polar Bear and Lamp Bottle:* One of the most attractive animal bottles. The white Milk Glass is of excellent quality. The bottle measures 11¼″ tall and is 3″ across the base, giving it a tall slender appearance.

242. *Sitting Bear Bottles:* These two old fellows are not made from the same mold although they are very similar. The white one is 11″ tall while the black one is 10¾″. They each measure 2¾″ across the front of the base. I have also found this bottle in an early, deep bottle green.

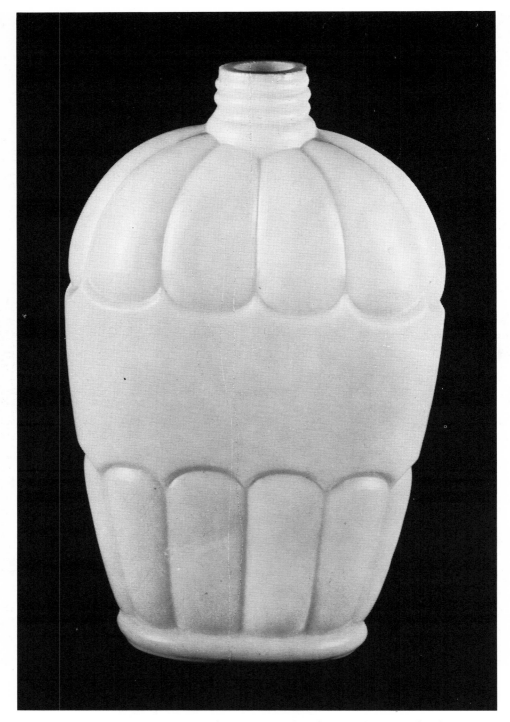

243. *Fluted Flask:* This is a very good looking whiskey flask. Its lines are simple but well proportioned. It is pint size, 7″ tall and 4¼″ across the widest part. A rare piece of good Milk Glass, wanted by bottle collectors as well as those interested in Milk Glass.

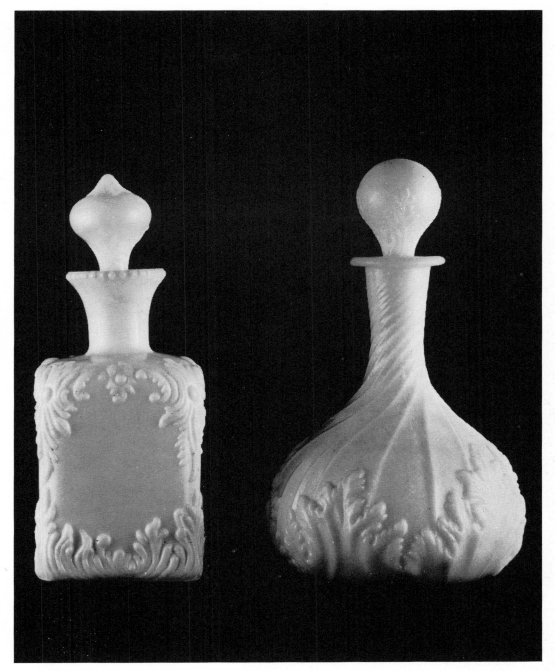

244. *Square and Round Milk Glass Dresser Bottles:* There were many dresser bottles manufactured in the 1890's and early 1900's. For the most part they were of inferior Milk Glass and looked worse for the paint applied to them. The two bottles shown are exceptionally good glass and well patterned. The square bottle called *Flame* had beautiful bunches of blue forget-me-nots centered in the four panels. The round bottle is called *Leaf.*

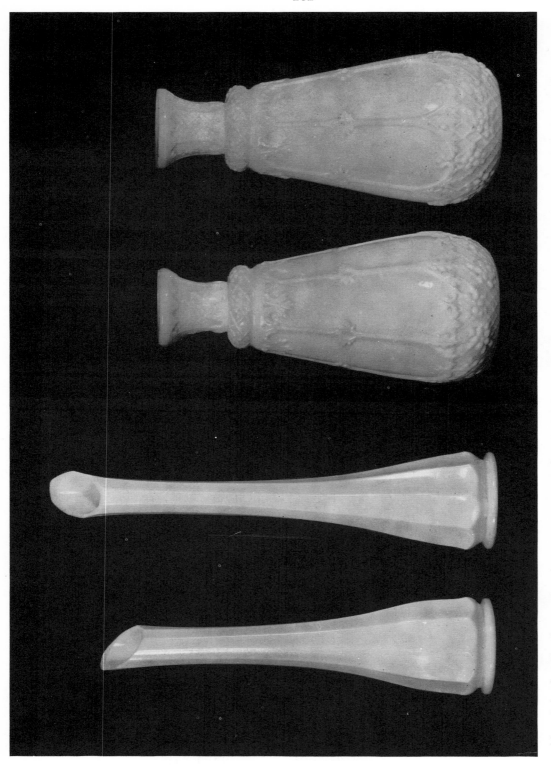

245a. *Pair of Milk Glass Bud Vases:* Only 1½" difference in height of the two vases. The taller is 14¼". They make a striking pair. They are fairly late, about the 1890's. 245b. *Pair of Conventional* *Vases:* Can be found in both milk white and blue. Millard calls them *Paneled Grape Vases* which I assume is a typographical error—there are no grapes.

246. *Pair of Rose Pattern Vases:* This pair of Rose pattern vases is fairly respectable looking after the gilt paint has been removed. They came in four different sizes. Those illustrated are slightly over 7″ tall and 5″ across at the widest point. Still plentiful in the antique shops if you can recognize the Milk Glass under the various paint and gilt disguises.

247. *Poppy and Rose Patterns in Vases:* These were of the same late period of manufacture as the Rose pattern vases. Both were turned out in quantity around 1910. They were lavishly painted.

248a. *Pair of Milk White Whiskey Bottles:* Identical except for the label imprint in the glass surface. 8¼″ tall by 4¾″ at the base. Excellent quality white Milk Glass. 248b. *Pair of Gar-land Urns:* Not old—25 or 30 years at most. Very faint garland-of-flowers design just under the rounded top rim. Detail of mold marking is very faint also.

*249. *Tall Grape Vases:* This pair of tall Grape pattern vases is outstanding because of size. They are about the largest pair of Milk Glass vases I know of, measuring 10¼″ in height and 6″ across at the widest part. Little is known about their early ancestry but they seem to be of the 1890 period. In recent years they have been reproduced by Westmoreland. *From the collection of Mr. and Mrs. E. W. Coble, Waterville, Ohio.*

250. *Pitcher Shape Vase:* The nationality of this beautiful Milk Glass Vase is a mystery. The manner in which the early handle is applied would indicate American manufacture. The etched design and the shape give it a European touch. The paint colors are black and gilt. The base was a separate piece of glass annealed to the bowl-like body. The base has a pontil mark which indicates this to be a blown piece of glass, not pressed. On the bottom, in red painted letters, is the word *Mast.* It is 12″ tall, 6½″ wide across the center and 4¼″ thick.

Chapter Ten

Reproductions

I CONSIDER THIS the most important chapter of the book. The ability to recognize reproductions, to distinguish them from originals, the knowledge of what is being reproduced and what is likely to be reproduced, and the evaluation of contemporary products whether reproductions or originals are of the greatest concern to both collector and dealer.

There are good reproductions and poor reproductions. Some are made so skillfully that only the most experienced dealers and collectors can detect them. Others are crude and easily recognized.

There are ethical manufacturers of reproductions whose aim is to manufacture beautiful pieces of glass for the department store and gift shop trade, and who have no intention of selling their reproductions to antique dealers to be pawned off as originals. Then there are the manufacturers whose primary interest is sales—the means by which such sales are obtained are immaterial. And there are a few unscrupulous dealers who, knowing fully the nature of the product, nevertheless offer it to the unwary collector as an original.

The average antique dealer is a pretty busy individual, scouring the country for antiques to supply customers' wants, keeping his shop in order, waiting on customers and learning as much as he can about the antiques he handles. Few have the time or opportunity to learn all the reproductions on the market, from student lamps to Milk Glass and from furniture to insurance calendar Currier and Ives masquerading in old mahogany frames. It is easy to see why the honest dealer is disturbed about reproductions. His lot could be eased greatly if all manufacturers of reproductions would mark their products in some manner to distinguish them from the early pieces.

Probably the best-known glass factory in the country today producing both clear pressed glass and Milk Glass reproductions is the Westmoreland Glass Company of Grapeville, Pa. The quality of its glass is excellent, its mold workmanship is unsurpassed and the finished product worthy of the highest praise. Westmoreland is not a newcomer to the Milk Glass field. The company was founded in October, 1889, and without interruption has continued ever since to produce fine handmade glass.

The location of the plant was selected because natural gas was available. The intense heat generated by natural gas gives a lustre and brilliancy to glass which never could be obtained by the old wood fuel method. Westmoreland Milk Glass reproductions are made by the same methods, the same formulae, in some of the same ovens and by descendants of many of the original workmen. In such an atmosphere of tradition and association it is understandable that they produce such fine handmade Milk Glass reproductions. Certain pieces are exact copies of early American originals, while others are continued production of Westmoreland's own creations from 1889 on. One outstanding copy is that of an imported French piece, a tall good-looking old rooster, no longer available from its European source.

It most certainly is not the intent of

this firm to foist either reproductions or imitations on the antique dealers or collectors. Its business is with department stores and leading gift shops throughout the country to whom it sells the choice handmade Milk Glass reproductions and original pieces of its own design. I have been informed that Westmoreland intends to mark all future production of Milk Glass with either a *W* or a *W G*. This is a forward step of great importance to all collectors and dealers. Furthermore, it points the way for all other manufacturers of reproductions. This will create a tremendous amount of good will among the dealers and collectors and will prevent much of the confusion that has existed in the Milk Glass field. (There are an estimated 13,000 to 14,000 antique dealers in the United States and many times that number of collectors and interested people.)

One of the main objectives of this chapter is to show some of the outstanding pieces produced by Westmoreland. Only through the generous cooperation of the company executives and their advertising agency was this material made available.

After the reader has compared the photographs in this chapter with those of the remaining chapters, he will have to admit that, from pictures at least, it is most difficult to differentiate between antique and reproduction.

Westmoreland production of the finer Milk Glass pieces is limited. Factory facilities cannot keep up with the demand. Such beautiful handmade items are being produced that, in the author's opinion, these present-day Westmoreland pieces will be the heirlooms of generations to come.

Another manufacturer of Milk Glass reproductions is the John E. Kemple Glass Works, East Palestine, Ohio. John E. Kemple comes from a family long associated with the glass business. Mrs. Kemple is as familiar with the factory and all its processes as she is with her own kitchen. She is also one of the most informed Milk Glass collectors I have ever had the pleasure to meet. Over the years Mr. Kemple has collected approximately one hundred and fifty of the old pressed glass molds which he uses to make his Milk Glass reproductions. He has such well-known patterns as Beaded Jewel, Blackberry, Ivy in Snow, and a Moon and Star Variant. He also has a plate mold for a rather unique bordered plate with the intriguing name, Lovers' Knot. He also has a limited assortment of dresser ornaments, including pin trays, puff boxes and several mugs, and some miscellaneous molds including a pair of Sawtooth candlesticks.

Unfortunately, this factory was discovered too late to prepare photographs of all the items produced there. Represented are his Blackberry, Beaded Jewel, and Ivy in the Snow pieces. The Kemple factory produces almost complete table settings in the Beaded Jewel pattern, Ivy in the Snow, and to a lesser degree in the Blackberry and Moon and Star Variant patterns.

John Kemple has one of the outstanding collections of old glass formulae. He very generously allowed me to examine them. Many of them were written in pencil on a plain sheet of paper and looked for all the world like Aunt Miralda's cake receipts except for the quantities: 1 ton of this and $\frac{1}{2}$ ton of that with 2 barrels of such and such thrown in to help the cause along. There were formulae for flint glass, opal glass, chocolate glass, ruby glass, slag glass, and many, many others. Some dated back to the early 1800's and others were some of the best of the '70s and '80s. These formulae had been handed down from father to son and from employer to employee.

Mr. Kemple sells his output mostly through two large distributing outlets, one covering the West Coast and the other the balance of the forty-eight states. The distributors sell to gift shops throughout the country and also to certain antique dealers.

I asked Mr. Kemple if he planned to mark

his glass so that it could be distinguished from antique pieces. He said, "No," and gave his reason: since his glass was made from original molds created prior to 1890, the pieces were not reproductions. If he were to put his name on the products, people would consider them modern pieces and it would curtail sales.

There is such a demand for Milk Glass at the present time, that with the right sales outlets the Kemple factory could sell its entire production, marked or unmarked. It most certainly would avoid a great deal of confusion if all Kemple pieces were marked in some manner to identify them as reproductions. They might even be marked *produced from the original molds.*

Westmoreland has signified its intention of marking all its Milk Glass. This leaves the Kemple factory and one other individual (name at present unknown), who owns a few molds, the only quantity sources of Milk Glass reproductions that are unmarked. It has been stated that the unknown is a jobber in the glass field. He is supposed to place his molds with a factory that will make glass for him and then he peddles his wares mostly to antique dealers who handle reproductions. This can be annoying but on such a scale can never seriously disrupt the antique glass market.

Knowledge of the background of the Kemple patterns should dispel whatever confusion exists.

1. Pattern Beaded Jewel, often called Lacy Dewdrop, was created in the 1880's as a pressed glass pattern by the George Duncan Glass Company of Pittsburgh, Pa. At that time it was made in clear glass only, not in milk white or any opaque glass colorings. About 1902 the molds were sold to the Co-operative Glass Company of Beaver Falls, Pa., and became their pattern No. 1902. In the 1920's the molds were again sold, this time to the Phoenix Glass Company of Monica, Pa., and called their pattern No.

800. Up to this time they were manufactured as clear glass. A little later the molds were acquired by H. M. Tuska, a glass jobber, who farmed them out to Westmoreland, where for the first time they were used to produce Milk Glass. I understand Westmoreland production was limited and soon the molds were returned to Mr. Tuska who eventually sold them to Mr. Kemple (about five years ago). Since that time the Kemple factory has turned out fair quantities of this pattern in Milk Glass.

This is a modern Milk Glass produced from old pressed glass molds.

2. The Kemple Blackberry pattern is another Milk Glass design being turned out from old molds. This pattern differs considerably from the early Milk Glass Blackberry pattern so much sought after by collectors. The berries in the Kemple product are very pointed, not oval in shape like the earlier pieces.

The Blackberry reproductions made by Mr. Kemple are of good quality Milk Glass —but from an antique collector's viewpoint are definitely not in the same category with the rare earlier pieces of the Oval Blackberry pattern.

3. A variety of Milk Glass pieces in the well-known Ivy in Snow pattern are being manufactured by Mr. Kemple from a set of the old Ivy in Snow original pressed glass molds also obtained from Mr. Tuska. Here again is a case where the molds were made for clear pressed glass originally, but have been producing Milk Glass during the past five years. It is an attractive pattern and Mr. Kemple is turning out beautiful pieces of Milk Glass—but again I must draw your attention to the fact that only in recent years has this pattern been made in Milk Glass.

4. The Moon and Star Variant as produced today by the Kemple factory should be fairly easily detected by collectors, because they should know from experience that this was not a Milk Glass pattern of early vintage. For several years I have heard rumors of this

Variant occasionally roaming the antique jungles, but never was I fortunate enough to flush one out until quite by accident I stumbled across its lair, the factory in East Palestine.

Products from these molds will eventually disappear from the market as the molds wear out, break or otherwise deteriorate. Several of the molds have already broken and are not being used at present.

Listed below are the Milk Glass plates, all by Westmoreland, known to have been reproduced up to the present time:

Plates

NAME	SIZE	NAME	SIZE
Three Kittens	7″, 8½″	Easter Chicks	7″, 8½″
Rabbit and Horseshoe	7″, 8½″	Beaded Loop Indian Head	7″, 8½″
Three Owls	7″, 8½″	Three Bears	7″, 8½″
Anchor and Yacht	7″, 8½″	Contrary Mule	7″, 8½″
Angel and Mandolin	7″, 8½″	Niagara Falls	7″, 8½″
Cupid and Psyche	7″, 8½″	Ancient Castle	7″, 8½″
George Washington	7″, 8½″	Beaded Border	6″, 7″, 8½″, 10½″, 15″

Open-Edge Plates

NAME	SIZE	SIZE OF ORIGINALS
Triple Forget-Me-Not Border	7″, 8″	7″, 8¼″, 9″
Lacy-Edge Border	11″	
Club and Shell Border	8″	7¼″, 8½″, 9″, 9½″
Square "S" Border	8½″	8″, 10″
Heart Shaped	8″	6″, 8″, 10″
Square Peg Border	8″	5″, 7″, 8¼″, 9″
Fleur de Lis Flag and Eagles Border	7″	7″
Wicket-Edge Border	9″	7″, 7½″, 8″, 8½″, 9″
Fleur de Lis Border	7″	7¼″

Westmoreland advertises: "Because these reproductions are from original molds, some of which are more than fifty years old, they vary in size—ranging from 7″ to 8½″."

This being so, it is easy to see the difficulty of telling the old from the new.

The open-edge plates are being reproduced in one size only. Since the originals were made in several sizes ranging from 5″ to 10″ (the square "S" plate reached this size), all other sizes found in these nine patterns must be early pieces.

The Lacy-Edge Border 11″ plate is a Westmoreland creation and was not of early origin.

This completes the listing of Milk Glass plates that have been reproduced up to date. Plates other than those listed are not reproductions.

CANDLESTICKS AND LAMPS

During the last few years the market has been flooded with all manner of Milk Glass lamps and shades. For the most part they have little true resemblance to the early Milk Glass pieces and even an amateur collector should be able to tell them on sight. I believe I am safe in saying that as far as reproductions in Milk Glass lamps are concerned they are not a serious problem to the well-versed collector.

There is one group of lamps that might cause some confusion, namely the lamps with Milk Glass bases and clear or colored glass bowl tops. A number of these have been reproduced, but they can usually be detected by the new connecting brass collar combining the Milk Glass base with the glass bowl. The brass burner connection on the top of the bowls where the chimney or electric connections fit is also new shiny brass which is a dead giveaway.

In candlesticks, the outstanding Milk Glass reproductions are Westmoreland's copy of the Hexagon base with Petal Top Dolphins. The reproductions come in two sizes, 4″ and 9″ tall. The reproductions are good-looking, but a close examination shows their late ancestry.

John Kemple has the molds for a pair of Sawtooth candlesticks which he makes in excellent quality Milk Glass. I have seen them quoted recently in antique shops and antique shows for as high as $35.00 a pair. In gift shops they sell for $2.50 and $3.50 a pair.

There are numerous other modern Milk Glass candlesticks — easily identified if studied carefully. I suggest that if you are really interested in seeing what is new in Milk Glass candlesticks and other recent productions, visit the glassware department of the nearest department store or gift shop and obtain the latest circulars put out by the Milk Glass manufacturers.

TRAYS AND PLATTERS

I know of no recent reproductions of Milk Glass platters. For some reason the manufacturers just haven't seen fit to copy any of the early ones or create any new items. In a recent circular Westmoreland does show one small ash tray called "Chick Ash Tray." John Kemple has a few old molds for small and medium dresser and pin trays. Reproduced in fair quantity, these are being sold to the gift shop trade and antique dealers who handle reproductions.

PITCHERS, CREAMERS, SYRUP JUGS

Reproductions of pitchers, creamers and syrup jugs also seem to be limited. The few outstanding examples are the Blackberry water pitcher, Budded Ivy water pitcher, and Block and Fan Variant two-quart water pitcher by Westmoreland.

The several small creamers manufactured by Westmoreland are Swan and Cat Tails creamer, Block and Fan Variant, No. 500 creamer, Peacock covered creamer, Floral Design creamer and Cherry Pattern creamer. Kemple produces the Beaded jewel pattern in almost all pieces including a creamer, and also a Pointed Blackberry creamer.

I know of no special reproductions of syrup jugs worthy of attention.

BOWLS AND COMPOTES

Keep your eyes peeled for reproductions of bowls and compotes, of which there are plenty of new pieces on the market. The great majority can be detected with little trouble, once you know what to look for.

The following are all reproduced by Westmoreland, except for the last two.

PATTERN	ITEM	SIZE
English Hob Nail	Rose Bowl	4″
English Hob Nail	Round Compote	5″
English Hob Nail	Footed Ivy Bowl	6½″
English Hob Nail	Covered Candy Jar	
English Hob Nail	Covered Bon Bon	4½″
Ribbed	Covered Cheese	

Open Circle Edge	Belled Bowl	9"
Lacy-Edge	Rose Bowl	6"
English Hob Nail	Point Bowl	
English Hob Nail	2 Handled Compote	8"
English Hob Nail	Crimped Oblong Bowl	12"
Open Circle Edge	Low Bowl	8"
Open Circle Edge	Footed Belled Bowl	10"
Fruit Pattern	Bowl	10"
Canoe Bowl	Bowl	7" x 13½"
Dolphin Base	Compote	7" and 11"
Thin Open Circle	Footed Bowl	10"
Open Circle	Footed Cupped Bowl	10"
Thin Open Circle	Footed Belled Bowl	12"
Ribbed Compote	Footed Covered Compote	
Lacy-Edge	Rectangular Bowl	
Ball and Chain Edge	Bowl	8"
Dolphin Shell	Footed Compote	8"
Block and Fan Variant	Square Covered Compote	
Beaded Jewel	Covered Compote (Kemple)	
Beaded Jewel	Covered Compote on Standard (Kemple)	
Moon and Star Variant	Open Bowl (Kemple)	
Ivy in Snow	Compote (Kemple)	
Blackberry	Compote (Kemple)	

COVERED DISHES, ANIMALS, HENS, ETC.

There are not as many of the covered animal, hen and duck dishes reproduced as the average collector believes. As you look over the list below you will see how few, comparatively, covered animal dishes are being manufactured today or were produced during recent years.

PATTERN	ITEM	MANUFACTURER
Mule-Eared Rabbit	Covered Dish	Westmoreland
	Coarse Rib Base	
Hen on Basket	Covered Dish	Westmoreland
3 sizes	Basket Type Base	
Tall Rooster	Covered Dish	Westmoreland
Atterbury Duck	Covered Dish	Unknown
Purple Slag Hen	Covered Dish	Unknown
	Basket Type Base	
Camel	Covered Dish	Westmoreland
Sitting Frog	Covered Dish	Vallerystahl
Basket with Hen Cover	Covered Dish	Westmoreland
	Basket Weave Handled Base	
Rooster on Ribbed Base	Covered Dish	Westmoreland
	Ribbed Base	
Swan with Raised Wings	Covered Dish	Westmoreland
	Lacy-Edge Base	

PATTERN	ITEM	MANUFACTURER
Cat	Covered Dish Ribbed Base	Unknown
Dog	Covered Dish Ribbed Base	Unknown
Robin on Pedestal Nest	Covered Dish	Westmoreland
Large Fish	Covered Dish	Vallerystahl
Large Turtle	Covered Dish	Vallerystahl
Scotty Dog	Covered Dish	Marked "Made in U.S.A."
Scotty Dog	Covered Dish	Vallerystahl
McKee Turkey	Covered Dish	Unknown

Here are some details concerning the above reproductions.

The Mule-Eared Rabbit on the coarse ribbed base is an old Westmoreland piece which is still being manufactured. It comes with decorated eyes and ears or plain. Any with painted pink lining in the ears you know are new, for the early ones did not have pink paint. It is more difficult to distinguish the new unpainted pieces from the old.

The best way to spot one of the three sizes of a Westmoreland Covered Hen dish is to look for the bright red paint atop the heads, and the painted eyes. The old hens did not have this fire-chief red used today. Of course, if the paint has been worn or scraped off, recognition is more difficult. But study the Westmoreland basket bases. The two larger hens have a rolled rope-edge base; the little one and the salt hen have a scalloped rim base.

The Tall Rooster is an excellent Westmoreland copy of a French import. It comes either with a bright red or plain comb, also with yellow or plain feet. The painted pieces are obviously new; careful examination will disclose the youth of the plain pieces.

As far as I have been able to learn, all of the original Atterbury Ducks were stamped on the bottom of the base, with the patent date 1887. But not long ago, I stumbled across an all white Atterbury type Duck identical to the original but for the quality of the glass and the fact that there was no patent mark or date on the bottom of the base. Since I have heard of others, someone must be reproducing them. I believe they are being made in West Virginia.

There seems to be a reproduction of the rare Purple Slag Hen covered dish floating around. At least a dozen have popped up in the last six months, ranging in price from $6.50 to $15.00. The price should be the tip-off. The original was a product of Challinor, Taylor & Co. The reproduction is on a chain border base typical of Hens produced by Vallerystahl. The slag mix consists of various shadings of lavender, not a clear cut purple and white mix as it should be if it were an early American piece.

The Camel covered dish is a Vallerystahl original reproduced by Westmoreland. At its best it is not an early piece; I believe it first appeared on the market in the early 1920's as an import. I have seen this piece in many top collections and it usually brings a top asking price when found in antique shops.

The Sitting Frog is recognizable on sight as a late French import—a Vallerystahl piece: slippery Milk Glass with a bright, new-looking, glaze finish.

The little Hen covered two-handled basket is another Westmoreland piece, evidently one of their own creations of some years ago. The early specimens had paint or gilt decorations; the modern pieces are minus make-up.

The medium-sized straight sitting rooster with a bright red comb atop a plain ribbed base is a companion piece to the medium hen on the basket base produced by Westmoreland. It is marketed today through department stores and gift shops.

The beautiful large Swan with the raised wings atop the Atterbury type Lacy-Edge rectangular base is made by Westmoreland who will sell the base individually or with the Swan top. The early Swans normally had glass eyes; the modern pieces have small painted eyes.

The small Cat covered dishes of the 5½" size on the ribbed bases have been recently turning up in rather large numbers. I do not know who is making them, but the sudden increase in the quantity available would indicate reproductions.

Similar to the above is the 5½" Dog covered dish on the ribbed base. These animals came in white, blue, and part white and part blue. It is rumored that these are being manufactured today, but I have no definite proof of their source.

The Robin on Pedestal Nest is being manufactured in limited quantities and retails for $10.00. The original was a Vallerystahl piece of which Westmoreland had done an excellent reproduction in both white and blue Milk Glass. The originals were white but there were a few blue marked "Made in France."

The sizable covered fish dish by Vallerystahl is so new looking, so slippery, and has such a bright glaze that the reproductions can be recognized at sight.

The Vallerystahl Covered Turtle is also so obviously modern that no one would purchase it as an antique.

The Scotty Dog round covered dish 6½" tall is so new it has stamped on the bottom of the base "Made in U. S. of America."

The McKee Turkey is being reproduced without the McKee name on bottom of the base.

If there are any other reproductions among the covered animal dishes, they are unknown to me at this writing.

MISCELLANEOUS

These are the known reproductions in this classification, all made by Westmoreland.

PATTERN	ITEM	SIZE
English Hob Nail	Tall Handled Basket	6"
English Hob Nail	Handled Oblong Basket	7"
Rooster	Egg Cups	
Rooster	Sherbet	
English Hob Nail	4-piece Condiment Set	
Shell	Nappy	6"
Open Circle	Footed Banana Bowl	11"
Open Circle	Cake Salver	11"
Double Hand	Tray	
Shell	Tray	6"
Leaf	Tray	6", 9", 12"
English Hob Nail	3-piece Condiment Set	
English Hob Nail	Goblet	
Uncle Sam Hat	Match Holder	
English Hob Nail	Bottle with Stopper	
Pansy	Dish	
Swan	Toothpick Holder	
Owl	Match Holder	
Duck	Open Salt	
Fruit	Goblet	

In addition to the above are various small gadgets readily recognized as spurious by the experienced dealer or collector. They are of no greater value and scarcely cause a ripple of confusion in the antique business.

SUGAR BOWLS

Very few of the really old sugar bowls have been reproduced. The few that have been are of no serious threat to dealers or collectors. I am listing the small group I have encountered, all made by Westmoreland:

PATTERN	ITEM
Block and Fan Variant	Sugar Bowl
Flower Design	Handled Sugar
Peacock	Covered Sugar
Cherry Design	Covered Sugar
Wide-Ribbed Design	Covered Sugar

John Kemple makes sugar bowls in the following patterns: Lacy Dewdrop (Beaded Jewel), Ivy in Snow and Blackberry.

BOTTLES AND VASES

I know of no really early bottles that are being reproduced. Westmoreland has one dresser bottle in the English Hob Nail pattern that is new, not a reproduction. Other than that, old Milk Glass bottles seem a safe field for exploration for the amateur—he won't be bitten by a reproduction bottle in the collectors' jungle.

Vases are a somewhat different story, for there are a handful of new and reproduced vases on the market. I am listing the more prominent ones below, all made by Westmoreland.

PATTERN	ITEM	SIZE
Block and Fan Variant	Vase	
Lily of the Valley	Vase	6½"
Swan and Cat Tails	Vase	7"
Grape	Vase	10"
Horn	Vase	7"
Flower	Vase	9½"
Colonial	Vase	
Hand Vase	Vase	
Wild Rose (Painted)	Vase	
Vase (Gold Decoration)	Vase	

CARAMEL GLASS AND PURPLE SLAG

The only two pieces of reproduced Purple Slag I know of are the large Covered Hen on the 7" Basket Weave base, evidently of foreign manufacture. This hen is described in further detail earlier in this chapter under covered animal reproductions.

The Daisy and Button baby shoe has put in an appearance. It is a poor reproduction, being more of a lavender-white mixture than the good old white-and-purple mixture of the slag or marble pieces. The manufacturer seems off on his mix and the result is more a mauve than a Purple Slag.

As far as is known, no Chocolate or Caramel Glass has been reproduced up to the present time.

251a. *Fleur de Lis, Flag and Eagles: 7″.*
251b. *Club, Shell and Loop Plate: 8″, white.*
251c. *Triple Forget-Me-Not Plate: 8″, white.*

251d. *Open Circle Border Plate: 11″, white.*
251e. *Fleur de Lis Border Plate: 7″. Original is 7¼″.* 251f. *Square Peg Plate: 7″, white. West-moreland Photographs.*

252b. *Wicket Edge Plate: 9″* white. 252a. *Square "S" Border Plate: 8½″*, white. 252c. *English Hob Nail Crimped Bowl:* 252d. *Crimped Oblong Bowl: 12″.* 252e. *Fan and* *Circle Bowl.* 252f. *Golden Wedding Covered Compote:* Plain Milk Glass, or gilt or colored grapes. Westmoreland Photographs.

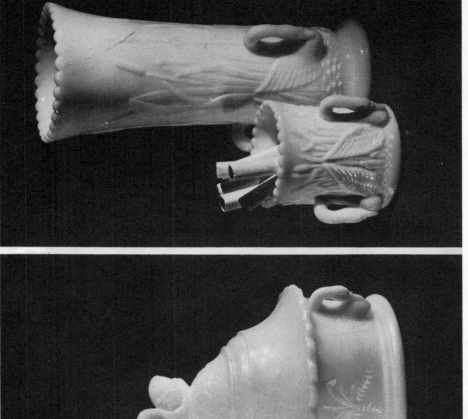

253a. *Ribbed Sugar:* There were a number of old Milk Glass pieces with this ribbed pattern so that this piece has been considered a safe collector's item. However, it is a Westmoreland reproduction as modern as yesterday. 253b. *Swan and Fern Butter:* The Swan pattern butter with the triple Swan decoration is often found in Purple Slag as well as in white Milk Glass. It was a popular pattern especially in sugars, butters and creamers. An excellent Westmoreland reproduction. 235c, d. *Swan and Cat Tails Match Holder and Celery:* Westmoreland reproductions of important Swan pieces. Westmoreland Photographs.

254a. *Swan and Cat Tails Sugar and Creamer:* The Westmoreland treatment of this popular and graceful pattern. Milk white. 254b. *Swan* *and Cat Tails Celery, Sugar and Creamer:* Additional example of Westmoreland's famous Swan pattern. Westmoreland Photographs.

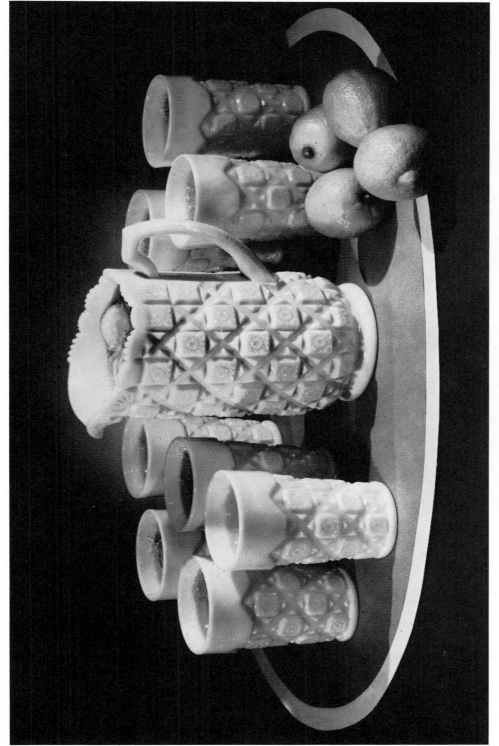

255. *Block and Fan Variant—Westmoreland No. 500:* This Block and Fan Variant pattern by Westmoreland is good-looking Milk Glass and one of the most popular on the market today. Westmoreland Photograph.

256. *English Hob Nail Punch Bowl:* This large English Hob Nail punch bowl, atop its sturdy base and surrounded by its well-shaped mugs is a handsome piece, reproduction or original. Westmoreland Photograph.

257a. *Hexagon Base Dolphin Candlesticks:* Also produced in black Milk Glass by Westmoreland. You will never find any antique Dolphin candlesticks in black. 257b. *Fruit Goblets:* Original Westmoreland pieces. Westmoreland Photographs.

258. *Westmoreland Decorated Vases:* Two modern vases, representing Bristol Glass, not Milk Glass, by Westmoreland. Westmoreland Photograph.

285

259a. *Blackberry Pitcher:* The berries in this piece are pointed instead of oval or round as in the earliest Blackberry pattern. Manufactured by the John E. Kemple Glass Works Co. 259b. *Ivy-in-Snow Water Pitcher:* A good-looking reproduction from an original pressed glass mold now owned by John E. Kemple.

260. *Shell Bowl, Dolphin Base:* Even the severest Milk Glass critics would have to acknowledge the appeal of this Shell and Dolphin compote created by Westmoreland. One of these compotes flanked by a pair of Dolphin candlesticks could be center motif for many attractive table settings. Westmoreland uses this Dolphin base for several bowl and Dolphin combinations. Westmoreland Photograph.

261. *Open Circle 10″ Footed Belled Bowl:* That modern Milk Glass as well as antique Milk Glass can be very attractive is proved by this piece. The modern Westmoreland footed bowl shown here is moderately priced. Westmoreland Photograph.

262. *Open Circle 12" Footed Belled Compote:* One of the largest of the modern Milk Glass compotes, measuring 12" across. Everything about this bowl or compote fairly shouts its Westmoreland origin. The base is found on most Westmoreland footed pieces, and the open circle edge is almost a Westmoreland trademark. Westmoreland Photograph.

263. *China Cabinet of Westmoreland Reproductions:* Truly a lovely display of Milk Glass. Although these pieces are not antiques they may be admired for their grace, beauty and charm. Westmoreland Photograph.

264. *Beaded Border Plate:* Westmoreland makes this in 6″, 7″, 8½″, 10½″ and 15″. It comes with painted fruit center, with plain centers and painted beaded border, in plain milk. With a coral beaded border it is called the Duchess of Windsor pattern. Westmoreland Photograph.

265. *Ball and Chain Edge Compote*: The sides of the original of this bowl are straight. The Westmoreland reproduction shown above has a flared top or border. Westmoreland Photograph.

266a. *Leaf Trays or Bon Bon Dishes:* Westmoreland created this original design based on an old pattern. 6″, 9″, and 12″. 266b. *Heart Shaped Plate:* Westmoreland No. 32, milk white, 8″. Westmoreland Photographs.

267. *Robin on Pedestal Base Blue:* The original of this beautiful piece of Milk Glass was created by Vallerystahl and came in white Milk Glass only. The equally good-looking reproduction by Westmoreland comes in blue or white. Westmoreland Photograph.

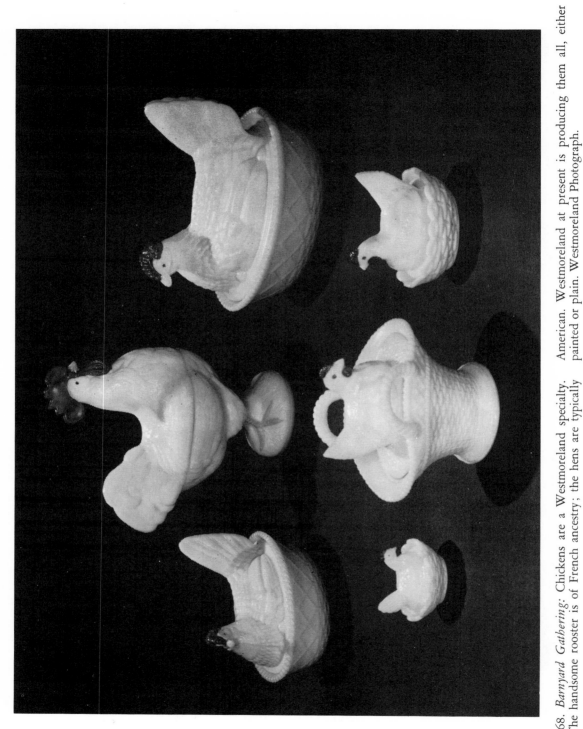

268. *Barnyard Gathering:* Chickens are a Westmoreland specialty. American. Westmoreland at present is producing them all, either The handsome rooster is of French ancestry; the hens are typically painted or plain. Westmoreland Photograph.

269. *Swan with Raised Wings:* The original Raised Wings Swan was an Atterbury product. The reproduction is a Westmoreland product. The original came with or without glass eyes. The modern version has small painted eyes. The antique model sells for as high as $50.00, the reproduction for less than $10.00. They both sit atop Lacy-Edge rectangular bases. Examine this piece carefully before you pay a fancy price. Westmoreland Photograph.

270. *Beaded Jewel Covered Butter:* The market is literally flooded with reproductions in this pattern. You will find large compotes, small compotes, bowls, footed bowls, creamers, water pitchers, sugars, butters and others. This is one of the four set patterns produced by the John Kemple Glass Works. If you intend to confine your collection to true antiques, remember this pattern.

THREE KITTENS

RABBIT and HORSESHOE

THREE OWLS

ANCHOR and YACHT

ANGEL and HARP

UPID and PSYCHE

GEORGE WASHINGTON

EASTER CHICKS

BEADED LOOP, INDIAN HEAD

THREE BEARS

CONTRARY MULE

NIAGARA FALLS

ANCIENT CASTLE

271. *Baker's Dozen by Westmoreland:* Thirteen novelty plates being reproduced by Westmoreland from the original molds. I believe that many collectors and dealers alike will be astonished to learn that these plates are being reproduced today by this well-known company. When I saw this advertisement I was startled to learn that the George Washington plate was again in production. These plates range in size from 7″ to 8½″ depending on the original mold size. The price should interest you—these are made to retail at about $18.00 a dozen. Electrotype furnished by Westmoreland.

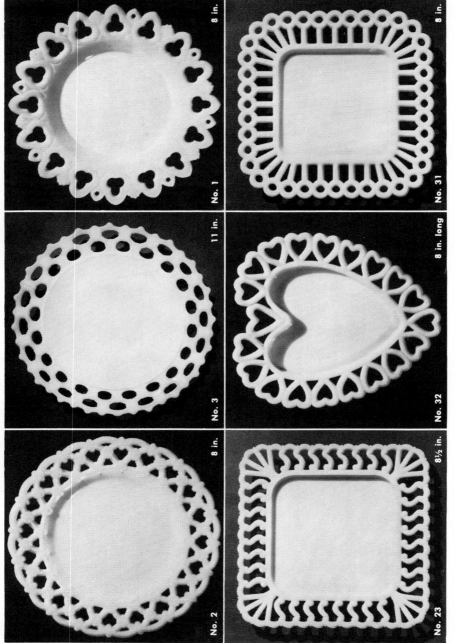

272. *Lacy-Edge Plates by Westmoreland:* Westmoreland's Lacy-Edge or open-work border plates. Note the sizes of the reproductions, then check the various sizes of the antique plates. Those sizes not reproduced are safe antiques. These illustrations show not only the Lacy-Edge plates being reproduced by Westmoreland, but indicate the excellent workmanship in the products of this company. Electrotype furnished by Westmoreland.

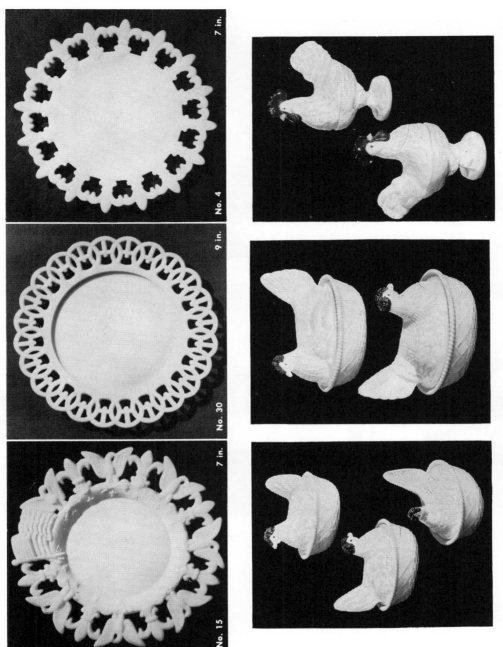

273. *Westmoreland Plates and Covered Bowls:* Electrotype furnished by Westmoreland.

274. *Westmoreland Reproductions:* Electrotype furnished by Westmoreland.

Chapter Eleven

Caramel Glass and Custard Glass

CARAMEL GLASS, originally called Chocolate Glass, was originated by the late Jacob Rosenthal and manufactured at the Indiana Tumbler and Goblet Co., Greentown, Indiana between November, 1900 and June, 1903. It has a rich creamed coffee appearance, with considerable variation in the coffee coloring caused primarily by the thickness of the glass. Thin pieces are much darker in color and are more uniform in shade. The thicker or heavier pieces are lighter in shade on the inside surface and darker on the outside surface. Tops are light compared with the bases, which are much deeper in chocolate tone.

The reason for the brief period of production was not lack of sales or popularity of Caramel Glass. Its acceptance upon being introduced at the Buffalo Exposition in May, 1901 was better than anticipated, so that the demand for this glass was never completely filled. However, on June 13, 1903 the factory at Greentown was burned out. Subsequently a few pieces were produced at the Fenton Art Glass Company, then dropped. As far as I know that is all the Caramel Glass made in the United States.

The leading designer of this glass was Charles E. Beam and some of the outstanding specimens which he originated are: Wicker Hamper with Catshead Cover, Caramel Covered Hen on Basket Weave Base, Covered Bird Dish (bird has berry in mouth), Flat-Eared Rabbit Covered Dish, Frog on Split Ribbed Base, Admiral Dewey on Ribbed Base, Dolphin Covered Dish (with fish finial on cover).

Frank Jackson, who later replaced Mr. Beam, was responsible for many Caramel Glass pieces.

The term "Slag" in conjunction with Caramel or Chocolate Glass is definitely a misnomer and should be abandoned. The product was neither a slag nor an accidental discovery. It was actually a flint glass formula created by Mr. Rosenthal.

CUSTARD GLASS

The name Custard Glass is derived from the custard-like color which varied from a drab, uninteresting yellow to a light, creamy, almost lemon shade of yellow. Custard Glass is usually very ornately decorated, with plenty of gilt, dark green or both.

This glass appears to have been created in 1886 by Harry Northwood at La Belle Glass Works, Bridgeport, Ohio. From this date until 1913 Northwood designed, manufactured and distributed Custard Glass through various companies with which he was connected. Some of his pieces are marked on the bottom of the base with the word *Northwood,* others with an underscored *N* in a circle. These are more valuable collector's items than the unmarked pieces made by Northwood or other manufacturers.

Many of the Custard Glass pieces I have observed looked as though they had come from the factory the very morning they were found. The gilt on the feet and decorated designs appear startlingly new-looking. Whether or not this is because the pieces in question have been well kept by their owners, or that the manufacturer had a special treatment that made the gilt last longer, is open to question.

275. *Paneled Water Pitcher:* Caramel Glass showing graduations of coloring from creamy coffee at top to almost creamless coffee brown at base. Handle is much lighter than lower two-thirds pitcher. 8¾″ tall, 4¼″ across the base

276. *Cactus Compote, Tumbler and Cracker Jar Base:* Three excellent studies in the ever popular Caramel Glass Cactus pattern. Original pattern designs were very limited in Caramel Glass. All told there were probably not more than a dozen. There were numerous oddities, but few actual patterns collectible in sets. Manufactured by the Indiana Tumbler and Goblet Co., Greentown Indiana. *From the collection of I. M. Wiese, Silver Mines, Conn.*

277a, b. Tumbler and mug in well-known Cactus Pattern. 277c. Caramel Shell and Leaf Tray: This smart looking Caramel Glass tray is 11" long and 5½" wide across the middle. Light creamy coffee color on the inside, it is a luscious caramel brown outside. This Shell and Leaf pattern is another collectible in sets. Made by Indiana Tumbler and Goblet Co.

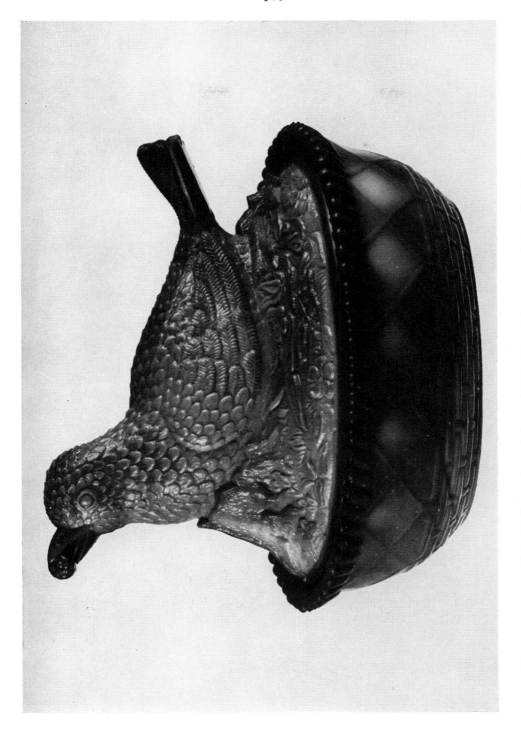

278. *Bird with Berry Covered Caramel Dish:* One of the rarest and most desirable pieces produced in Caramel Glass. Another product of the Indiana Tumbler and Goblet Co.

279. *Caramel Glass Hen:* A very rare piece credited to the artistry of Charles E. Beam and made by the Indiana Tumbler and Goblet Co. Look closely at the scalloped detail of the hen's tail feathers which are a particular feature of the hens produced at Greentown. Even this Caramel Glass Hen has a touch of gilt here and there. *From the collection of Mr. Roland E. Deitemeyer, Toledo, Ohio.*

280. *Chrysanthemum Sprig Water Pitcher:* This Northwood Custard Glass pitcher is usually painted gold, green and pink. However, the one above is free of such adornment. I have also seen this pitcher with the Northwood mark on its base. The glass coloring is an odd pale greenish yellow. Size, 8¾" tall and a full 5½" across the base.

281. *Argonaut Shell, Water Pitcher and Tumblers:* This large water pitcher in the rare Argonaut pattern is one of the best looking pieces found in Custard Glass. It is marked Northwood piece. Its dark green seaweed and coral, and gilt colored shells are still brightly painted. The gold bands around the tumblers are well preserved and the yellow coloring of the Custard Glass itself is above average. I have also found this pitcher in blue clear glass with opalescent rims on top and base. *From the collection of Mrs. Maude M. Haley, Toledo, Ohio.*

282. *Winged Scroll Bowl and Sauces:* This set is as new looking as the day it left the factory at Indiana, Pa. It had been stored away and never used—the gold on it is as bright and shiny as a newly minted dime. The Custard Glass is a creamy hard-sauce-yellow. Incidentally, the gold is the only painted decoration. There are none of the usual greens or pinks. The legs are gold, the flowers and leaves are gold and all is topped off with a bright gold rim decoration. *From the collection of Mrs. Bessie B. Mollard, Zelienople, Pa.*

283. *Golden Daisy and Rose Custard Sugar and Creamer:* Gold and green make up the color scheme of this ornate Custard Glass sugar and creamer. The green is considerably lighter than the dark green found in the Argonaut pattern. As you will note from the picture, the paint work on these two pieces is as good as new. The flamboyant decoration is typical of Custard Glass ornamentation. *From the collection of Mrs. Bessie B. Mollard, Zelienople, Pa.*

Chapter Twelve

Purple Slag (Marble Glass)

NOT TOO MUCH is known about the manufacture and production of Marble Glass or Purple Slag. Challinor, Taylor and Company of Tarentum, Pa. are said to have been the largest American producers of this glass. It is also known that a considerable quantity of our finer pieces of Marble Glass were imported from England. Many pieces can still be found with English registry marks on the bottom.

There are various slag mixtures to be found in glass—purple, blue, green, orange and not infrequently a molasses or butterscotch color. I have heard the blue and green mixtures referred to as Canadian Glass. Of course, this is inaccurate. The glass must have originated in England and then it must have been sent to Canada. Some imaginative soul gave it a Canadian birthright.

The blue or green Slag mixtures are rare and are probably of English origin. The molasses or butterscotch mixtures were most likely made both in this country and in England. I have seen this color with and without the English registry mark.

The original name for this glass was Mosaic, but has long since been changed to Marble Glass or Slag. These Marble or Slag mixes are sometimes wrongfully called "end-of-day" pieces. Only last week I asked a dealer if she had any Slag or Marble Glass and she said, "No, but I have a swell end-of-day piece," and she proceeded to bring forth a lovely Purple Slag celery.

Almost all Slag items are scarce today and the really choice pieces bring record prices. It would be rather difficult to acquire a complete table setting in any single pattern except at a fabulous cost, after considerable travel and hunting.

Many of the pieces to be found in Purple Slag are also available in white Milk Glass, and occasionally they are repeated from clear pressed glass patterns. In my own wanderings I have found identical pieces in Purple Slag, milk white and in blue clear pressed glass.

There were numerous gadgets, trinkets and small items, from soap dishes to match holders and from toothpick containers to rose bowls for the collector to gather.

Since the quality of Marble Glass varies considerably, I doubt that all, or even a large proportion, of the American product was produced at one factory. I know that a considerable amount was produced by Challinor, Taylor. You can almost spot one of their pieces at sight. However, I don't believe they would want to claim credit for some of the apologies for Slag or Marble that can be found.

There appear to be three distinct types of Slag. The first is the open-mix, where there is a definite line of demarkation between the white Milk Glass and the purple glass. Second, the fused-mix, well blended together, like a thoroughly mixed marble cake batter that shows a distinction of white and purple, but not in great separate masses. Third, the over-mix where the white seems to lose its identity and become all purple with occasional glimpses of almost clear glass in the finished product.

The English pieces show yet another combination of white and purple, a much darker glass to begin with, and a very neat blending of white and purple in more equal proportions of each color. The detail of the English is far superior to that of the American.

There is one final group that has also been called Marble Glass. In it are the marble-like Hens pictured in illustration 144 and the two sugar bowls in illustration 231. Although these pieces are referred to as Marble Glass both by Millard and by this author in previous chapters, they are not to be considered in the same category as the Slag pieces in this chapter. Those pieces were predominantly white Milk Glass with a small amount of coloring added to the mix, nor the over-all mix used in the Slag described in this chapter.

284. *Closed Lattice Edge Plate:* Here is one of the aristocrats of the glass plate world. Approximately 10½″ in diameter. The marble effect in each plate is entirely different, even when the plates were made by a single glass worker from the same batch of glass. They vary considerably in shading and mixture from light to dark and from white to deep purple.

285. *Shell Variant Covered Dish:* This is a really beautiful piece of Purple Slag even though the marble effect is not distinct. It is a full 8″ in length, 6¾″ across from rim tip to rim tip, and 5″ tall to top of shell finial. On the inside of the cover, underneath the rim, and entirely covering the base is an unusual basket design. The shell motif decorates the four corners of the cover.

286. *Rain Drop Water Pitcher:* Rain Drop is a rare pattern in Purple Slag. This lovely water pitcher shows the pattern detail to advantage. The pitcher is 8″ tall to the curl of the lip, slightly over 4½″ wide at the base, and a bit over 5″ across the top. More of a mauve color-ing than a sharp purple and white contrasting effect. The Rain Drops appear on the handle as well as in a ring around the base. The body is completely covered with round knobs represent-ing Rain Drops.

287a. *Flower and Panel Water Pitcher*: This pattern appears on five pieces, covered butter, creamer, spooner and quart water pitcher. Produced by Challinor, Taylor and Co. 287b. *Dart Bar Water Pitcher*: This Dart Bar pattern can be found in various set pieces, as pitchers, bowls and tumblers. Whoever produced this pattern was certainly not expert in the art of making Slag. The pitcher is 8¼" tall at the lip and 4¼" wide at the base.

288a. *Sun Flower Creamers:* A rare and beautifully executed design.   288b. *Holly Sugar Bowl
Base:* Made in England, has a true craftsman's
touch. A magnifying glass will show all the details.   288c. *Acorn Pitcher:* So like B in detail
and coloring that it must assuredly come from
the same factory.

289a. *Fluted Silver Pickle Jar:* The combination of Purple Slag and silver is rare. This is one of the few such combination I have encountered in years of collecting. The top half is fluted, the lower half base is composed of alternating blocks and cut squares. Height, 8″; height of silver frame, 11¾″.

289b. *Block Daisy Pitcher:* This good-looking Purple Slag pitcher has touches of blue in its upper half. The lower half with the Block Daisy design is good purple and white Slag mix. American, 5½″ tall by 3″ across the base. A rare pattern.

289c. *Dart Bar Cake Stand:* This piece measures a full 11″ across the top and stands 6″ tall. The marble is good mix and it has one dash of a brilliant blue on the top surface. Most Purple Slag cake stands are of plain design.

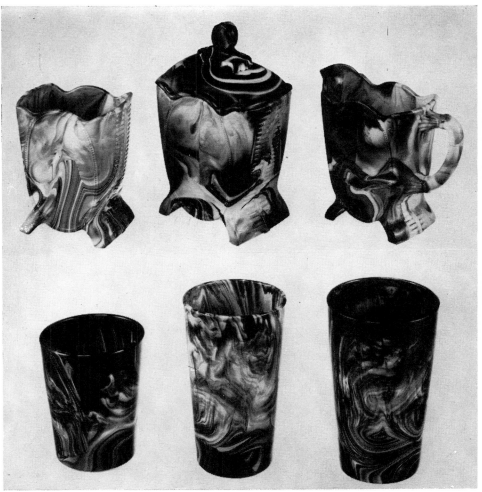

290a, b. *Swan Pitcher, Low Dish:* The pitcher on the left is brown Slag, the low dish on the right is Purple Slag. Both appear to be American pieces—the marble effect is typically American. 290c, d, e. *Oval Medallion Square Set:* In this Oval Medallion creamer, sugar and spooner there is almost the full range of marble effect. 290f, g, h. *Three English Tumblers:* Each of these English pieces has a registry mark on its base. The taller ones have a marked bluish coloring in their upper halves, a color often encountered. The tallest tumbler is 5″ tall, the smallest, only 3½″.

291a. *Leaf Paneled Bowl:* Centered at the base of each of the fifteen panels is an elongated leaf design.   291b, c. *Pair of Notched Platters:* 13″ long, nearly 9½″ wide at center. Both top and bottom view. Coloring is blueberry blue. 291d, e. *Two Dart Bar Bowls:* About half the pieces found in this pattern are poorly mixed. Large bowl, 8″, small bowl, 5¾″.

292a, b. *Basket Weave and Fan Oblong Trays:* Design is entirely on sides and bottoms. The main bottom motif, which you cannot see in the picture, is a pair of open fans end to end. Approximately 8″ by 5½″. 292c, d. *Pair of Rain Drop Bowls:* Design is on the underside of each bowl. Coloring is on the darkish side, but swirls of lighter streaks float through the pattern giving the bowls almost a deep sunset coloring. They are 8¾″ across the top, only 2¼″ deep. 292e, f, g. *Two Ringed Urns and a Match Holder:* E and G, 2½″ tall by a scant 2″ across the top. F, good design detail, 3″ by 1¾″ by 2.

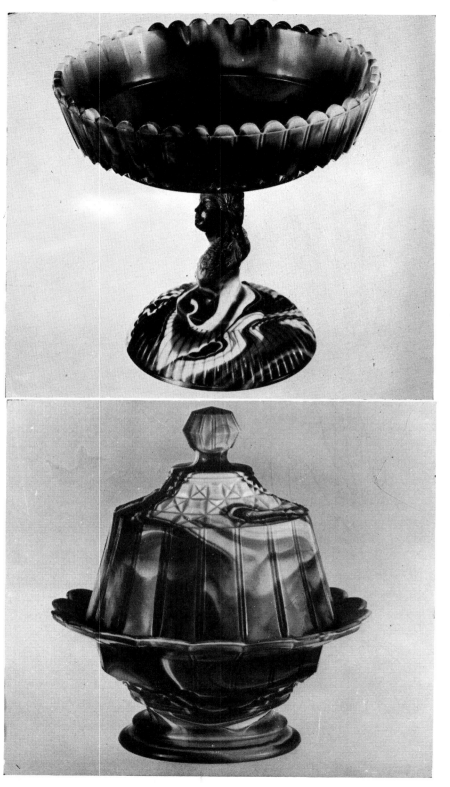

293a. *Jenny Lind Compote:* This piece is made of excellent quality Slag glass. Nearly 7½″ tall, 8½″ across the top bowl and 5″ across the ribbed base. 293b. *Fluted Covered Butter:* This fluted design is one of the few Purple Slag patterns available in a variety of pieces. The pattern is always made of top quality glass. It is 8″ tall to top of knob on the cover and 7¼″ wide from tip to tip of scalloped rim.

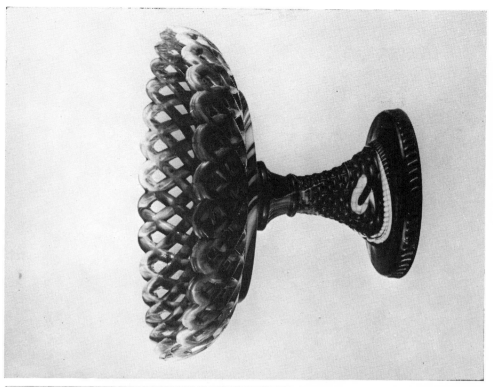

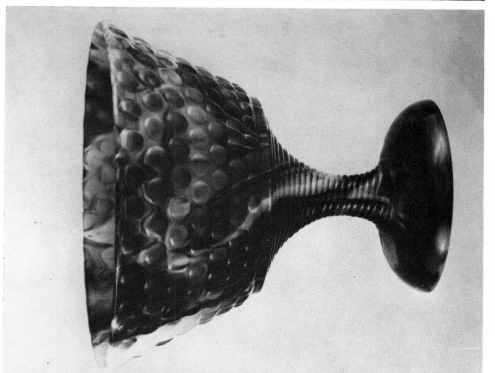

294a. *Large Rain Drop Open Compote:* One of the handsomest of the Rain Drop pieces is this Swirl Column base compote. It measures slightly over 7½″ tall and is a full 8″ across the open bowl. 294b. *Closed Lattice-Edge Basket Stem Compote:* A collector's piece and well worthy of the honor. The bottom of the bowl matches the base in coloring. The bottom surface of the bowl features the basket weave design found on the base column. The marble effect is superb. The bowl is 9¼″ across, nearly 6½″ tall and the base is 4½″.

295a. *Fluted Celery:* These Fluted celeries are much in demand and always bring top prices. They measure 8¼″ tall, and stand on a 3¼″ base. 295b. *Jewel Celery:* This is found in other Milk Glass colors as well as Purple Slag (see Chapter VII), and is considered rare in any color or type of glass. 8½″ tall, with a base slightly more than 4¼″ wide. 295c. *Ribbed Leaf Celery:* The design detail, the proportions, the general shape make this English celery an outstanding piece. It measures almost 9½″ tall with a base of nearly 4″.

296a. *Flower and Panel Covered Sugar and Spooner:* Always popular and any pieces in this design bring good prices. Occasionally, you will find specimens in brown Slag. 296b, c, d. *Two Wee Vases and a Miniature Pitcher:* B looks like a parfait glass. 5¼″ tall, 1¾″ wide at top. D is but 4¾″ tall with a 2¼″ base. C is just 3½″ tall, with a 2″ base.

297a, b. *Ruffled-Edge Low Dish and Crimped-Edge Candy Dish.* 297c, d, e. *Two Small Urns and a Footed Kettle:* Urns are 3½″ tall, 3¾″ wide. Kettle is English, 4″ wide, 2½″ high.

297f, g, h. *Two Match Holders ana a Barrel Tumbler:* F is 3¼″ tall with 3½″ base. H is 4″ tall with 2¼″ base. G is 4″ tall, 3¼″ across center.

298a, b. *Double Basket and Small Vase:* The lower half of the basket is blue Slag, the upper half and the handles are purple on the outside. Inside the entire basket is Purple Slag. It measures 5¼″ tall to top of handles, the base is 1¾″ across. The small vase is 4″ tall and slightly over 2″ across its beaded base 298c, d, e. *Two Mugs and a Ten-Paneled Tumbler:* The mug on the left has a tremendous amount of detail on each side. The center cup is larger and of a good Slag mix, as is the ten-paneled tumbler on the right.

Index